W9-ABO-783

Municipal Knowledge Series

Cultural Planning

for *Creative Communities*

GORD HUME

*with contributions from Greg Baeker, Nancy Duxbury, and Tim Jones
and a foreword by Glen Murray*

brought to you by the publishers of

Municipal World
CANADA'S MUNICIPAL MAGAZINE

Markham Public Library
3201 Bur Oak Avenue
Markham, ON L6B 0T2

©Municipal World Inc., 2009

All rights reserved. No part of this publication may be reproduced, stored in a retrieval system, or transmitted, in any form or by any means, photocopying, electronic, mechanical recording, or otherwise, without the prior written permission of the copyright holder.

Library and Archives Canada Cataloguing in Publication

Hume, Gord

Cultural planning for creative communities / Gord Hume.

(Municipal knowledge series)

Includes bibliographical references.

ISBN 978-0-919779-89-1

1. City planning--Canada. 2. Cultural industries--Canada--Planning.
3. Creative thinking--Canada. 4. Urban renewal--Canada.
5. Art and state--Canada. 6. Canada--Cultural policy.
7. Community life--Canada.

I. Title. II. Series: Municipal knowledge series

NX750.C3H84 2009   307.1'20971   C2008-907625-7

Published in Canada by
Municipal World Inc.
Box 399, Station Main
St. Thomas, Ontario N5P 3V3
(Union, Ontario N0L 2L0)
2009
mwadmin@municipalworld.com
www.municipalworld.com

ITEM 0035
Municipal World — Reg. T.M. in Canada, Municipal World Inc.

Printed on

CONTENTS

Foreword. . . . . *v*

Chapter 1   Municipal Cultural Planning. 1

Chapter 2   Cultural Planning for a
Changing World 7

Chapter 3   Developing Your Cultural Plan. 15

Chapter 4   Cultural Mapping 29

Chapter 5   Economic Development 35

Chapter 6   Downtown Revitalization and
Heritage Properties 49

Chapter 7   Development Partnerships and
Opportunities. 61

Chapter 8   Planning and Placemaking Tools 67

Chapter 9   Public Art 75

Chapter 10   Social, Environmental, and
Community Challenges. 79

Chapter 11   Changing the Thinking 87

Chapter 12   Strategic Planning, Priorities, and
Success Indicators. 95

Chapter 13   Culture and Sustainable Development –
A Global Perspective on our Future . . 103

Chapter 14   Case Studies 111

Appendix   Ideas for More Information, Funding,
and Help 123

References. 125

About the Contributors 127

On the Cover

Ribbon of Friendship – Vision Corridor
Windsor, Ontario

Reaching out across the world in a gesture of friendship, this sculpture was a gift from Yin Xiaofeng of China to the people of the City of Windsor. As our two worlds connect with one another in friendship, this sculpture honours those individuals who make the effort to understand each other and embrace our differences.

Photographer – Kimberly Hurst

Foreword

by Glen Murray

Cultural Planning for Creative Communities addresses the value and centrality of culture to community building in Canada. This book is a first in our country, and provides important insights and practical "how-to" information for municipalities, cultural groups, heritage advocates, arts leaders, politicians, planners, and everyone interested in building strong, prosperous, and culturally-vigorous communities. Arguably, its most significant contribution will be the understanding it offers of the relationship between culture and creativity. Culture is a placemaker, and is the underpinning of all the activities we define as creative. It contributes to the physical beauty of a place, the capacity for civility, inquiry, and pluralism, expressions of authenticity, and finally the values that keep a place welcoming, fluid, inclusive, and entrepreneurial.

Creativity is central to the capacity of what my friend Jane Jacobs often identified as the most important job of the city: generating wealth. If cities cannot do their job in wealth generation, they cannot do many of the other jobs they need to do to serve their citizens.

The culture of a place and people is about three cultures: culture as values; culture as urban vibe; and culture as a formal artistic expression. Small "c" culture is our values and beliefs, and informs our lived culture, the aroma, sound, look, feel, and touch of our street corners, cafes, subway platforms, and parks, and the vibe and buzz of neighbourhood main streets and gathering places. This lived culture is canvas on which the bright colours of our expressed culture are applied: the great galleries, museums, public art, and signature buildings that become the iconic brands of urban centres. These characteristics are critical to attracting the most important resource of a modern economy – creative people.

Canadian communities are experiencing the shift from industrial economies dependent on manufacturing and requiring proximity to resources
and trade routes, to creative regional economies dependent on concen-
trations of skilled people and driven by innovation.

We don't have to look far outside our borders to see the role culture
and creativity plays in sustaining and facilitating the rebirth of communities. Pittsburgh saw over 250,000 jobs lost as every single steel mill
closed in the mid-1980s, yet it emerged with the leading life sciences
business cluster on the eastern seaboard, and became a cultural mecca
with the development of the Warhol Museum and a rebirth of its downtown. Long suffering Reykjavik, where the planes don't stop to refuel
anymore and the cod fishery collapsed, has emerged as an innovation
and cultural powerhouse with a dynamic range of cultural assets, including three major public art galleries, globally-focused educational
and research facilities, and public infrastructure that can only be described as public art. Reykjavik should continue to be more resilient
than other cities, even in the face of yet another onslaught of severe
global challenges. Creative urban regeneration in the long run allows
cities – even small, isolated ones – to endure and eventually to ride out
the global economic tides.

Innovation depends on people and on the rapidity with which their
ideas and research can be commercialized. The success of communities
depends on their ability to apply new knowledge to production, technology, culture, placemaking, and human development. Creative people
– the Creative Class – are not only the source of culture; they are the
foundation that determines the enduring strength of regions. Innovation
has surpassed production as the fundamental source of wealth in this
global economy. The diversity and depth of a local culture is, in turn,
one of the most powerful magnets for a creative workforce.

But, this doesn't happen by osmosis, and this book provides insight on
how to prime the Cultural Planning pump to move culture to the centre
of overall community building. This requires us to see every infrastructure investment and development not only as an economic or environmental asset, but as a cultural asset. Bridges, for example, spur investment, open up lands for development, and expedite trade and transportation. But, they are also art; they connect water, land, and sky; they
connect people and culture – as well as the past to the future. Bridges
can be iconic symbols of a place like the Golden Gate Bridge in San
Francisco; they can be the very soul of commerce, culture, and exchange, like the Ponte Vecchio in Florence; and they can even be the

focal point of political controversy and debate over the very identity of a place, like the Esplanade Riel in Winnipeg. But, they are all undeniably cultural.

Integrating planning involves the melding of social, cultural, environmental, and economic policies into a coherent and coordinated framework with clearly delineated wealth-generating objectives. This is critical to successful communities. Co-locating the right mix of assets, investments, and institutions can create significant economic multipliers that will drive the value of land and buildings, increase economic activity, and build a community's tax base.

But, this is about more than culture of economy; finding the soul of any community can be difficult, but the journey is also part of the reward. In a time of increasing public concern over the traditional infrastructure needs of municipalities, we need to remember that we must also build a cultural infrastructure as part of the heart of our communities.

We also need to understand that governments at all levels need to change their traditional ways of doing business. The status quo is not acceptable. The needs of the people and our communities are in the 21st century; too many government practices are rooted in the 19th century.

"Creative City" concepts offer a really exciting new opportunity to build neighbourhoods, reinvigorate downtowns, fortify arts organizations, develop robust local economies, strengthen cultural facilities, celebrate a rejuvenation of our community spirit, and develop an irresistible, fresh, clear vision for our future.

Let me commend the authors of this much needed book. They are all acknowledged leaders and experts in their field, and this book will provide a most welcome addition to government practice in our country, as well as internationally.

Several of Canada's leading municipalities have or are adopting integrated environmental, cultural, social, and economic municipal plans. In the next few years, many Canadian municipalities will do so. Cultural plans are an integral part of such an integrated plan. It is a challenging, but exciting time for municipal leaders.

Becoming a Creative Community is a worthwhile goal for progressive municipalities. Attracting and retaining the Creative Class is paramount in developing a strong and sustainable local economy. That means we need to build different kinds of communities to succeed in the future, and we need to do that now.

Goddess of Winged Victory, Toronto – photo by Slava Poliakov

This book is about how to create, develop, and implement this new way of thinking and acting for local councils and their communities, whether they are a town or a
vast metropolitan region – they can become a Creative
Community by using "Creative City" concepts.

Chapter 1

Municipal Cultural Planning

"If creative cities are the end, cultural planning is the means."
(Verwijnen and Lehovuori, 2002.)

Municipal Cultural Planning is about shaping, developing, and enhancing the economic future of your municipality. It is about place and placemaking. It is about identifying and harnessing all of the cultural assets and resources in your community. It is about strengthening and developing the arts and artisans. It is about changing how communities do business and make decisions. It is about becoming a Creative Community.

For Canadian municipalities, becoming a Creative Community is about leading the way in our rapidly changing society, as we respond to new demographic trends and rapidly shifting economic realities.

It is about jobs, prosperity, and the knowledge-based economy. It is about building and rebuilding municipalities that are livable, environmentally friendly, and appealing to today's knowledge workers, and to an increasingly diverse population mix.

And, it is about finding new ways to establish more cohesive and sustainable neighbourhoods in our towns and cities. It is about how to rebuild downtown cores that are often faltering. It is about the built and natural environments. It is about our civic heritage, and the future of our towns and cities.

The "Creative City" movement is being driven by local municipalities. Most senior levels of government have been slow to respond to this new, community-driven initiative. The leaders are local arts and cultural groups, heritage activists, councillors, architects and builders, senior municipal staff, emerging leaders, people interested in new ways of building more livable neighbourhoods, and bright young people moving to or staying in communities where their talents and lifestyles are welcomed and they can find fulfilling jobs in the modern economy – community leaders and community dreamers.

1

These are concepts that are important to municipalities of all sizes. "Creative City" (a term coined by social economist Richard Florida), should be thought of as a generic term, not as "urban only." Rural and smaller communities are just as affected by changes in municipal governance and economic pressures as any larger community. They can have just as much success implementing a Municipal Cultural Plan, and just as much success in becoming a Creative Community.

Towns and cities of all sizes are beginning to see the opportunities forged by new partnerships and economic development opportunities. They are also seeing the repercussions of municipalities that aren't offering the lifestyle, job opportunities, quality of life, and social environment that young graduates are seeking today.

From encouraging entrepreneurship to helping established companies grow and prosper, Canadian communities have enormous new challenges and responsibilities today. Wealth creation – that is, building local prosperity, not just redistributing the property tax base – is now a fundamental task.

Economic prosperity is being shaped by the knowledge-based economy. North American society, economics, and population trends are being turned on their heads by the changes in the traditional economy and municipal government. These are fundamental and systemic changes that simply cannot be ignored by any responsible municipal council. That's why Cultural Planning has become so important to civic government today.

The External Advisory Committee on Cities and Communities (the Harcourt Commission) was created by a former federal government to look at Canadian communities in 30 years time. In its 2006 report, the commission (building on the works of others, including Australian Jon Hawkes) confirmed the four "pillars of sustainability":

► economic prosperity;

► social equity;

► environmental sustainability; and

► cultural vitality.

The commission also noted crisply, "Creativity and innovation are together the overall elements to propel cities to success."

The evidence is simply overwhelming – to prosper in the future, Canadian communities must embrace Cultural Planning as a key and core element of municipal government.

2

The competitive reality is that most communities now offer similar amenities to potential investors and companies. They have serviced, zoned land available. They have wireless high-speed Internet. They have an economic development corporation of some kind that offers help to new businesses. What differentiates Canadian communities today is the quality of life they offer – and that does vary substantially.

Cultural Planning helps communities become, or remain, distinctive and unique. Becoming a Creative Community means protecting your unique heritage properties, having a throbbing downtown core, being appealing to entrepreneurs starting new businesses and generating new wealth. It means being a "Smart Community." It means respecting the environment. It means being innovative and progressive as a community. It means having "buzz."

The quality of life a community offers is often the most distinctive difference and a major deciding factor in where businesses will locate, or re-locate. The knowledge-based economy is driving our future wealth – and that is all about people, ideas, and technology. If your community isn't appealing as a place to live and do business, then your future economic prosperity is very much in doubt.

This book was written in response to many requests for help by municipal colleagues across the country. Every municipality is different, so there can be no template that fits every situation or case. That is a good thing, because it makes every Municipal Cultural Plan local, different, and unique. The process of developing the plan is consistent and structured, and this book offers specific ideas, direction, parameters, and assistance so that local towns and cities – communities large and small – will be able to develop and implement their own plan to become a Creative Community.

The "Creative City" movement is a relatively new function of local government that has evolved in only the past few years. In this book, we have pulled together many "best practices" from cities and towns of all sizes in Canada as examples for other communities. Great creativity and energy are coming from many of our municipalities, and Canada has been recognized as something of a leader.

I am particularly grateful to four of my friends and colleagues, who have been among the pioneers in the Cultural Planning field in Canada, and who have each graciously contributed an important chapter to this book.

Glen Murray, who had a resplendent career as mayor of Winnipeg and now heads up the Canadian Urban Institute, has been one of the early proponents of Cultural Planning across Canada.

Greg Baeker has done some brilliant research and has written Municipal Cultural Plans for leading municipalities such as Toronto, and is a leading expert in the Cultural Mapping exercise for AuthentiCity. He consults for municipalities across Canada.

Tim Jones heads ArtScape, a wonderfully innovative Toronto company that has put together some remarkable public-private partnerships that are changing neighbourhoods, and proving that Cultural Planning does work.

Nancy Duxbury is based in Vancouver, where she helped to start the Creative City Network of Canada, and now is the Executive Director of the Centre of Expertise on Culture and Communities at Simon Fraser University.

In the interests of full disclosure, it is important to note that all of the authors have many affiliations, and are involved with many prominent organizations. This book represents the views or policies of no particular institution or organization, and represents solely the work and views of the authors. To be specific, at the time of writing, I am a member of city council in London, Ontario, chair that city's "Creative City" committee, and chair the Ontario Municipal Cultural Planning Partnership; this book is independent of all of them.

When I led London's "Creative City Task Force," which started in 2004, there wasn't much case work or experience in Canada to help. So, we plunged ahead on our own and pioneered some ways of doing Cultural Planning, and recommending things to council. This book will reference those experiences from time to time – not to brag about what we did, but to help you with the goods and bads of your own municipal process based upon the hard realities of what we learned. Without question, the "Creative City" movement has advanced in the past five years, as has the methodology and sophistication of the research, reports, and recommendations.

What hasn't changed is the fundamental need by municipalities to change. Cities need to embrace "Creative City" principles in their normal course of business – concepts such as more sustainable growth patterns and neighbourhood development, attracting and retaining creative people, and focusing on the knowledge-based economy.

For some municipalities, this will be a revolution; for some, an evolution. But, the status quo is not acceptable for communities that want to prosper and grow in the future.

We have tried to put together a "how-to" book for you, but we can't overemphasize that your community is unique, and you need to do the things that are necessary for your community to show off its unique strengths, heritage, and characteristics. These are guidelines, suggestions, and ideas for you. There are no rigid lines, which is also one of the things that make the "Creative City" concepts so much fun and so exciting to so many.

When I was asked by Fresno, California to help them start their "Creative City" task force, their outcomes and goals were quite different from those I observed, for example, when I addressed the Vaughan council about their city. But, the principles and the parameters for Municipal Cultural Planning are the same, and the process is what this book will assist you in understanding and developing.

It is a rare opportunity to recognize and then lead fundamental change for a community. That is a privilege that comes to elected officials, senior administrators, and community leaders very infrequently. Cultural Planning offers that unique circumstance; communities that are smart enough to embrace change and lead innovation are going to be the successes of the future.

I am grateful for the many communities that have shown leadership in this area, and have graciously invited me to speak, or to exchange ideas, share concepts, and develop unique and interesting best practices for local government. I am greatly impressed by the innovation, creativity, and commitment that contribute to the significant local achievements by so many elected and administrative officials in towns and cities across Canada. It is exciting to see.

Cultural Planning is now firmly entrenched as the fourth pillar of good local government. It joins the economic, social, and environmental pillars of sustainable communities. *How* we do it will shape our cities for decades to come.

If we do it, it will affect local economies and economic prosperity. But, if communities choose *not* to recognize and respond to "Creative City" concepts, then those consequences, too, will be substantial. Bright young people are not going to be attracted to communities that don't offer the environment, job opportunities, social experiences, and quality of life that they expect and demand today. The inevitable result will be stagnation and economic decline.

Workers in today's knowledge-based economy are highly mobile and their skills move with them. Whether it is computer software designers, engineers, musicians, artisans, writers, research scientists, academics, · or anyone else in the creative industries, they are highly prized by prosperous and successful municipalities.

Canada is almost unique among nations today because we enjoy many prized resources: ample space as a country; water and agricultural products; a progressive social structure; a safe and secure nation; and unparalleled opportunities for young people to grow and develop in our increasingly diverse country.

Cultural Planning for Creative Communities is the first Canadian publication written for and directed at Canadian municipalities to deal with these new and emerging challenges.

What is especially exciting is that the next stages of Cultural Planning – whatever innovative and exciting ideas they may be – are already being contemplated by smart communities, by innovative municipalities, by community groups demanding and leading change, by young students who will graduate years into the future, and by arts, cultural, and heritage activists who are saying, "We can build a better community."

It is in the cities and towns across Canada where innovation is taking place; wealth is being created; art is being produced; world-leading research is happening in laboratories; medical and scientific achievements are being celebrated; a new generation of sculptors and musicians is being developed; new neighbourhoods are being built; and old neighbourhoods are being revitalized.

It is an enormously exciting time for local governments to show their leadership and to create their communities of tomorrow. We won't do this by thinking small, by allowing council debates to focus on minor flaps instead of major projects, by having small minds elected to do small things.

This book is also a call to action; municipalities must better assert themselves with the other orders of government. It will require momentum for change, goodwill, and respect at all levels, and a determination by municipal leaders to affirm their expanding and critical role in the economic development of our nation.

Chapter 2

Cultural Planning for a Changing World

The facts are overwhelming:

➤ 80 percent of Canadians now live in urban areas;

➤ according to the 2006 Census, 5+ million residents of Canada are non-white or non-Caucasian, and they overwhelmingly live in large cities;

➤ over 40 percent of the populations of Toronto and Vancouver are visible minorities;

➤ our population is aging;

➤ our economy continues to shift from industrial to knowledge-based enterprises, with corresponding growth of the workforce in that sector;

➤ environmental issues and concerns are now a worldwide priority; and

➤ Canada is arguably becoming the most diverse country in the world.

In other words, life in Canadian towns and cities is changing. Quickly. Profoundly. Irreversibly. The pace of change is accelerating.

These new realities are combining to present significant new challenges to municipal governments. Council members, mayors, and senior administrators are quickly realizing that the "old way" of doing business just doesn't work anymore.

Old thinking about economic development and a community's prosperity are not effective today. This confluence of events (such as demographic and immigration trends) and shifts (changing values, for example) are driving new ways of thinking at the local level. Municipalities that want to prosper are finding new ways of delivering their traditional services that range from installing the 311 phone service that lets its customers (i.e. taxpayers) do business with it 24/7, to rebuilding deteriorated downtowns into attractive, vibrant cores that appeal to the segment of the population that Richard Florida has called the Creative Class – an estimated one-third of the workforce that includes:

► creative professionals – the classic knowledge-based workers, including those working in healthcare, business and finance, the legal sector, and education; and

► super-creative core – including scientists, engineers, techies, innovators, and researchers, as well as artists, designers, writers, and musicians. (Florida.)

At its heart, this is what Creative Community planning and implementation is all about – changing a community, propelling it forward into the 21st century, and enabling it to become a leading municipality that will attract and retain bright young people who will be the leaders of tomorrow.

Cultural Planning recognizes that life in urban and rural areas is changing rapidly, and therefore municipal governments must do more than respond – they must lead. Cultural Planning is the process by which municipalities become Creative Communities.

"Creative City" thinking is a concept, not a size designation; smaller municipalities are just as involved with and have similar challenges and opportunities as any larger city. In other words, it's a way of thinking for municipal governments, not an urban versus rural, or large versus small issue. This book is about how to create, develop, and implement this new way of thinking and acting for local councils and their communities, whether they are a village or a vast metropolitan region – they can become a Creative Community by using "Creative City" concepts.

In 2004, London, Ontario became one of the first cities in Canada to research and then produce a comprehensive Cultural Plan – a "Creative City" plan. The chair of the task force that did the work summed up the report this way: "This report is about two things – the economic future and prosperity of our city, and changing how London thinks."

In other words, "Creative City" thinking is big. It deals with big issues, big changes, big concepts, and big future economic, social, and civic ideas and opportunities.

To deliver those kinds of changes takes many smaller pieces that must come together. That's where a well-researched, community-driven Cultural Plan can be so effective. That process will be driven by the local community and council.

Cultural Planning is a wide-ranging process, touching many parts of your community: accessibility issues; diversity; immigration patterns; foreign investment; social housing; service delivery; building neighbourhoods; public art; transit planning; urban design; and more.

That is also why it is so crucial for municipal councils and the local community to understand the scope that a Cultural Plan Report should cover. Sometimes, that's a problem because the old way of thinking and doing business in a municipality is just too narrow, too rooted in silos, and too traditional.

Creative enterprises and industries today are now driving much of our local economies. Communities of all sizes are impacted by this new reality. Just think about how many of these businesses are already part of your municipality, because these are some of the range of creative businesses today:

▶ college or university – from the professors to the students;

▶ medical research;

▶ artisans;

▶ engineers;

▶ sculptors;

▶ aeronautics;

▶ publishing companies;

▶ musicians;

▶ software developers;

▶ graphic designers;

▶ video game designers and manufacturers;

▶ marketing companies;

▶ writers;

▶ planners and urban designers;

▶ artists;

▶ high-tech manufacturing;

▶ bio-tech research and development;

▶ tech-transfer companies;

▶ chefs and food and wine industry experts;

▶ robotics;

- film makers;
- computer design, servicing, and teaching;
- audio and video recording;
- radio and television;
- fashion;
- cultural industries such as orchestras, museums, and theatres;
- environmental industries;
- newspapers and magazine publishing;
- aerospace;
- specialty manufacturing;
- hospitals;
- settlement agencies; and
- so many more!

In other words, creative industries already make up a substantial portion of your community's economy. This economic impact will only increase in the future, representing billions of dollars for local economies. The issue for municipalities then becomes, "How do we retain and attract more creative industries, because these are the jobs of the future?"

That means attracting the Creative Class. The people who work in these industries. The people who are innovative, creative, cutting edge, and original.

Businesses of all sizes are finding that attracting good employees is a huge challenge. In fact, the availability of talent (often from a college or university environment) is increasingly one of the key determining factors of where companies will set up or expand business. Companies demand a pool of educated, qualified workers. It is now a critical element of deciding where businesses will locate, or if they will stay in a community, expand their operations, and create more new jobs.

Why are these critical societal changes important to a municipal council? Simply because, more and more, we are in a society where the CRINK Economy is predominant. (CRINK is my admittedly inelegant acronym for the Creative-Innovative-Knowledge economy that now is such a dominant part of local economies.)

And, the people who make up the CRINK economy tend to be highly mobile; their greatest resources are their brains. They expect a certain kind of lifestyle, and they will have several jobs in their careers. They aren't anchored to any particular factory or office, laboratory or art studio, graphic design company or software producer.

Top economists disagree on how large the CRINK economy is, but reasonable estimates are that more than one-third of all jobs today are in the CRINK industries. Clearly and indisputably, the economic impact is in the trillions of dollars.

That's why this CRINK economy and the people working in it are crucial to prosperous, leading Canadian municipalities today, and for the future.

It is a hugely competitive environment for business to attract good employees. It is the number one issue for many businesses right now. Hiring is expensive, time consuming, and vitally important. Once a company hires good employees, the trick is to keep them happy, motivated, fulfilled, and employed.

And, there is a secondary problem – two income households. One spouse may be offered a great job, but if the other person in the relationship can't find an equally fulfilling career, the couple may not move. A university may offer a brilliant young researcher a fabulous job, but if her partner can't get a good job or doesn't like the community …

How is this new social engineering a municipality's problem? Simple. Among the most important aspects of attracting bright young people to a good job are the characteristics of the community in which they're going to live. One of the key elements of retaining good employees is the lifestyle that they and their family will enjoy.

From interesting housing opportunities to the physical environment, from the social, cultural, and arts opportunities to safe neighbourhoods, from quality infrastructure (roads, sewers, and safe water) to the technological infrastructure (fibre optics and wireless technology), municipalities have a critical role to play in helping companies grow and prosper.

Now, the circle is complete – because it is municipalities that have the responsibility for, and therefore must create (with many community partners), those livable communities. In other words, a progressive, robust, and safe community that offers great job opportunities with growing companies, comfortable and unique housing, a vibrant downtown, and an enjoyable lifestyle for its residents will prosper. This will be a community that includes a throbbing, contemporary arts and cultural

11

scene, sports and athletics for people of all ages, and all the other elements of a fun, dynamic community.

These are the communities that will attract the Creative Class, the jobs they do, and the businesses they create. These are the Creative Communities.

A community that is rooted in the past, that doesn't understand or respect the changing social climate, that has a rotting core, that is environmentally unfriendly, and that isn't responding to the new wants and needs of business and workers alike, is not going to prosper in the future.

What a council decides and then does about shaping and building the kind of livable community it can become has never been more important. That is why Cultural Planning has become such an important part of a modern, successful Canadian community today.

It is not a role that comes easily to some elected and appointed officials. It is a profound shift. Acknowledging the need to do municipal government in a different way is intimidating for many elected councillors. It is safer and more comfortable to keep on the same old path, approving the same old reports and recommendations. And, if the council members don't always "get" this new paradigm, certainly some voters don't either.

That is why leadership at the local level for Cultural Planning is so crucial – and often so difficult. This is a new and different path for local government. To be truly effective, Cultural Planning must permeate every aspect of a municipality's operation. From engineering to planning, from parks and recreation to by-law enforcement, staff must learn that "culture" is a positive in municipal planning and policy development; and culture is one of the keys to prosperity for any community.

What is particularly fascinating is that communities that *do* get it – that are changing, that are trying to build a better community – are often finding that the majority of the public are waiting for councillors to catch up. The people have already figured out that communities need to be environmentally responsible; to have clean, safe, and strong downtowns; to make neighbourhoods fun and livable for families; to provide attractive libraries, galleries, theatres, and stadiums; to offer walking and bike paths for families; to provide responsive public transportation; and to do civic planning on a human scale that recognizes that people come first. These people recognize that, at the end of the

12

day, a municipal government's greatest responsibility is to provide a safe, clean, and sustainable community for its citizens.

A Cultural Plan should be comprehensive in nature and bold in its thinking. It should look forward. It should offer hope and ideas and opportunities. It should appeal to the community and provide on-going opportunities for public involvement, ideas, and development. It should outline clearly just how a community is going to deliver that safe, clean, and livable community, and deliver a prosperous future in the CRINK economy.

A Cultural Plan is not the end of the Cultural Planning process, but rather the beginning. Canadian communities that have done this kind of plan have found that community groups embrace the report and its recommendations. Often, community groups will "claim" one or two of the recommendations and take possession of them – further enhancing and developing them, offering new ideas and thinking, and extending them into even more exciting directions.

Why would the London Home Builders Association form its own "Creative City Committee"? Simply because they realized that they were going to be the builders and developers of the neighbourhoods of the future. It was a brilliant move, and has driven new design and place-making ideas about different ways of designing neighbourhoods, building energy-efficient homes, and offering distinctive choices for consumers.

Cultural Planning is very much about partnerships. It is about planting seeds in a fertile municipal field. It is about having the community embrace a new vision and plan.

It is about Calgary and Vancouver stretching and beating out cities around the globe to host the Olympic Games, and then developing amazing Cultural Plans as part of these wonderful events.

It is about Orillia, Ontario, in 2006, publishing its Vision of Culture:

► We see a city in which culture is understood to be central to making Orillia a place where people want to live, work, play, and invest.

► We see a city that is a regional hub for tourism, built on the quality of its natural and cultural environment, and the vitality of its arts, heritage, and cultural activities.

► We see a city where growth and development are managed in a way that preserves the community's natural and cultural assets and its unique small-town ambience and identity.

13

► We see a city that values public space across the community, working to protect and enhance it through effective urban design, and art in public places.

► We see a city that supports and values a dynamic cultural sector of arts, heritage, and cultural organizations, and individuals committed to collaboration and shared resources.

It is about Trois Riviere, Quebec becoming the poetry capital of Canada.

It is about Waterloo, Ontario doing an extensive and valuable community inventory and mapping process for arts, culture, and heritage.

It is about Toronto linking with London, England to jointly discover shared opportunities for arts, culture, heritage, tourism, and more in a unique "Creative City" initiative.

It is about Winnipeg developing a strong, community-based public arts policy that has become a model for other cities.

It is about London, Ontario starting Canada's first-ever Creative City Committee of its city council to ensure the community recognizes the importance of Cultural Planning, and shaping a new kind of city by implementing its task force report and recommendations, and seeking new community ideas.

It is about Saint John, New Brunswick and Saskatoon, Saskatchewan – and so many places in between – that are taking steps to change, improve, and develop the creative side of their communities.

Canadian municipalities have rightly earned a reputation for innovation and community-based planning. The "Creative City" concepts are simply the next exciting and important step in improving Canadian municipalities – helping them become Creative Communities.

Chapter 3

Developing Your Cultural Plan

Developing your Cultural Plan is a crucial and fundamental first step.

The document will serve as a beacon around which the community can rally, and makes an unequivocal commitment to the "Creative City" principles.

It will express a philosophy, and make an important statement about your community as it is – and what you wish it to become.

It provides the foundation document for the next several years of development and progress, and provides a clear reference point for the public and for council.

It provides the policy foundation and framework that council can approve, and which then provides the civic administration with comfortable parameters within which to operate.

There are a number of important decisions that must be made as your community moves forward with researching, creating, and producing the report and its recommendations:

1. Who is Driving the Process?

Typically, there are three possible drivers for developing a Cultural Plan:

► the community, usually driven by a coalition from the arts, heritage, and cultural sectors;

► senior municipal administration, who may perceive a hole in the community's mosaic; or

► a politician who has become knowledgeable or interested in this part of a community's economic and social progress.

All can be effective, but the paths will be different.

Community-driven – Action will normally come from activist groups or leaders in the arts, cultural, and heritage sectors. Sometimes, it is driven by the sector's inability to have come together in the past, leaving a weak local arts council or sector. Sometimes, it is driven by arts groups demanding more active and tangible support for their work from their council, which usually has rebuffed them or provided only tepid support. Or, it may simply be a confluence of issues and concerns that coalesce into a desire to see a more creative, vibrant community.

Such a scenario will generally see the community group seek assistance from other municipalities that have done successful Cultural Plans. This will likely mean a presentation to council or a key civic committee, which will then take the recommendation forward for administrative input and eventual council approval.

Council members may or may not get it. It is unlikely all of them will. There is often some skepticism about community-driven initiatives around the council table. It is important to engage at least one member of council to help drive the agenda forward. It is also important to have strong staff support.

The report going to council should be clear in its objectives, timing, costs, process, and outcome. It must be general enough to allow some flexibility as the process proceeds, but defined sufficiently in its parameters and goals that council is comfortable.

One of the greatest challenges may well be to get the broad community and a majority of council members to recognize that there is a problem, and that change is therefore needed. Sometimes, there is a great sense of "comfort" in the status quo. There may be a reluctance to face the new and changing economic reality, and to make the social and cultural changes that are needed.

It will be crucial for the community group to make clear that this report is not just a way to get some additional funding for their own organizations. Instead, they must emphasize that this is a community-wide process that focuses on the economic prosperity that the council wants to see for the community.

One of the initial difficulties may be bringing together the traditional "arts community" and the traditional "business community." They may not immediately see the links to the new CRINK economy. There must be a clear acknowledgment that a big part of the Cultural Planning process is the economic development of the community.

Some communities have a series of "roundtables" or "open forums" to bring together diverse groups and ideas. These can help to shape a shared vision, and provide further impetus for initiating the Creative Community process. It is important to recognize new partnerships, alliances, and common goals because the process must be community-driven and broadly accepted.

It will be very important to give council "a win" in this process. Council must be seen to be providing leadership in an important new initiative for the community. The public must perceive that council is engaging the community for the benefit of the community. Local arts and cultural groups must put aside their own egos for the benefit of the community. Business groups must get on board. University and college presidents must be active supporters.

It may take some time and education to help the council and the community understand that "culture" is a strong, positive word that has a broader and more important definition than usual.

Culture is an economic driver. Culture is a community driver. Culture is a social driver.

One of the dangers at the early stage in this exciting process is it being casually dismissed as, "Oh, it's just those arts groups wanting money again ..." or "We can't afford to give culture money when we can't afford to fill potholes ..." or "Nobody cares about that old heritage building downtown ..."

You must make your council understand the economic significance of Cultural Planning. It is a major paradigm shift for many council members, and it can be a hard concept to grasp.

Developing a champion on council will pay significant dividends. The reason is simple: council members get to speak at the debate, and get to vote on the recommendation. Just as importantly, they have access to other council members. In a municipal council process that generally doesn't see party alliances at the local level, each vote at the council is a new opportunity for coalitions to form, agreements to be reached, and votes to be traded. And yes, that happens.

That's why it is also important to pack the gallery at the council meeting when the vote is being taken. And, be unanimous in the support of this process – there is no easier way for councils to get off the hook than having a divided community. Lobby in advance – politely send emails, talk to your local mayor and council members at civic events and functions, and make sure they know how important this is to the community's future. If local politicians think that there is a genuine ground-swell of support, they are more likely to look favourably on the initiative.

Administration-driven – This process will usually come from a municipal manager who has become involved with or aware of the benefits of
a Creative Community, often by attending conferences, hearing experts
speak on the "Creative City" concepts, or reading about successes in
other municipalities.

This will be more of a bottom-up bureaucratic process, and is a normal
procedure in municipalities. The difference here is that staff will need
to seek support from both the community and from politicians.

This is, however, a great opportunity for business, community, and cultural organizations to become involved with the process, and to be a
key part of it. It can open doors for arts groups at city hall, and get
some of the members of this community on the inside for a change.

Politically, council members may be more comfortable with receiving
background documentation and a budget and process outline from their
staff, which is a normal course of business for councils. While community support is always important, it may not be as crucial in this scenario as the preceding one.

The administrative report would outline the background, perhaps provide examples from other communities, detail the time line and the outcome expected, and the process would normally then be staff-driven. A
couple of council members would likely be seconded to the committee
or task force, as well as some community representatives. Administration would likely recommend hiring a consultant to assist in the process
and to help write the report.

Politically-driven – In this scenario, Cultural Planning comes from the
top down. A mayor or member of council who has become interested in
and engaged with the concept would most likely drive the process. It
could even start at the council level with a proposal or notice of motion
from the council member, asking for council agreement on the formation of a task force to research and prepare a Cultural Plan and Report.

Council could then refer the matter, and ask for a staff report outlining
the budget, process, and so on, or it could approve the request and au-
thorize some staff support. It would not be unusual for the council
member proposing the plan to be appointed chair of the group. The
council member would then work with the administration and reach out
to the community to form the task force.

The advantage to having a council member drive the process is that this
individual can continue to push from the inside, and will have the ear
of senior administration.

18

At some point early in this process, it may be useful to have a "community conversation" or "roundtable" to get input from the general community, particularly those involved with the creative industries. This could be a full-day discussion (perhaps on a Saturday), or a half-day seminar. What is important is to come out with an action plan to push the process to the council.

2. Forming the Process

One of the interesting early decisions that must be made is what kind of process do we intend to follow? Do we want a task force or a committee? Who's going to sit on it? What kind of budget do we require? Do we hire a consultant, or are we going to do this ourselves?

Council will need to know these answers before approving the process.

I must declare a definite preference for the task force concept. It implies a temporary piece of work that starts, and then at some point finishes, and then will disband. Many business people and arts and community leaders prefer that, rather than being appointed to another endless committee.

A task force also lets people focus on the specifics of the project, and not get diverted into troublesome side-issues. There is a certain sense of achievement and freedom that doesn't occur in the committee process, because members know their work is complete with the presentation of the report and recommendations. They aren't involved in the implementation. That can prompt even more innovative thinking.

A committee, almost by definition, will tend to be slower and more process-oriented. If the intention is to evolve from the committee preparing the report into a committee that then implements the recommendations under the guidance of the administration, then the process may work satisfactorily. The danger, however, is appearing to make the process too closed and cozy, where committee members may be accused of promoting their own interests.

There is no perfect process. But, there are some key parameters and guidelines that will help municipalities in doing this. One of these is having a strong chair.

There are going to be conflicting interests and positions amongst the task force members. There are going to be different opinions about the direction of the research and the recommendations. There are going to be strong political differences. There may well be social or other self-interests (more specifically, on behalf of a particular group or organization) that a task force member feels compelled to advance with some vigour. And, there may well be historic differences between and amongst members of the arts and cultural communities.

As well, the work of the task force may meet substantial negative response from a portion of the council and/or the community. This is not an easy or comfortable process because, to be effective, the task force must ask some hard questions about the community. And, when you ask the hard questions, you've got to be prepared for the tough answers.

An example: when London started its task force process, the city had a lingering issue that was a hang-over from a decade previously when a former mayor had refused to proclaim Gay Pride Week. The Human Rights Commission eventually found the mayor and city in breach of human rights legislation, and imposed a fine. London's task force had the courage to confront the issue, make a statement in the report, and subsequently talk quite openly about the importance of the gay, lesbian, bisexual, and transgender community to the city's creative future. Since then, the city's relationship with that community has improved dramatically, and a negative image of the city that had persisted in many communities across North America has been changed. However, not everyone in the city was supportive or enthusiastic about that. A strong chair needs to be prepared to both defend vigorously and proactively communicate issues and ideas coming from the task force.

Once the chair is selected, so must members of the task force. This can prove to be surprisingly difficult.

There are going to be a lot of different interests in the Creative Community process: economic; business; cultural; heritage; artistic; students; community; downtown; diversity; planning and by-law issues; developers; the arts business side; university and colleges.

This next statement is difficult and will cause some controversy – but sometimes you can't involve "the usual establishment."

Think this one through carefully. As much as the chair of the board of the orchestra (or theatre, or museum, or art gallery, or chamber of commerce, or labour council ...) may want to serve, maybe she or he just isn't right for the task force.

The "Creative City" concepts are new, bold, and innovative in nature. Task force members must check their egos at the door of the meeting room, and can't bring old battles and self-interests into a new war. Sometimes, the better answer is just not to let them in the room at all.

That means a task force of very bright people, often younger, and most of whom have never been involved in a municipal committee before. Radical? Yes. Effective? Absolutely.

Generally, asking a widely diverse group to serve on the task force will create a new dynamic that is healthy, refreshing, and different. They don't bring old baggage. They don't defend turf. They don't fight old battles.

Their thinking will be fresh and clear. Their focus will be on the future. They will look at community problems differently. They will offer innovative ideas to new challenges. They will likely reflect what your community wants to become.

In other words, you want the brightest people you can find. You want people for who they are, not for what it says on their business card. These people will often have diverse interests and will have knowledge of many different aspects of community life. They are most likely members of the Creative Class that you want your community to recruit and retain, and neither age, gender, nor (lack of) experience in civic issues matter in the slightest.

Two other notes on forming the task force. First, it is vital that the community be predominant. In London, we had three members of council and 13 members of the community. The message was clear – this was community-oriented. Vancouver followed this process as well – two council members and 11 community members, and their 2008 report sets out a clear vision for Vancouver's arts and cultural community plans and direction.

Second, to keep the "usual establishment" involved and informed (and supportive!), you may wish to establish a working group, perhaps consisting of the general managers of the top eight or 10 arts/cultural organizations in your community. They can provide valuable insight and research into issues that will arise during the task force's discussions, and will be particularly useful in helping to sell the report to their own organizations. The working group would be active partners in the work of the task force, but not voting members, because they could have a vested interest in decisions that might affect their organizations.

3. Operating the Task Force

A clever task force chair will soon recognize that it shouldn't be business in "the usual old way." The undoubtedly dynamic group that has been recruited and come together isn't interested in boring, routine, and long meetings.

While every community will be different and should develop its own process and procedures, perhaps some examples from London's experience will be helpful.

The first meeting was held in the council chambers where the new task force members met for the first time. In fact, for some of them, it was their first time ever in city hall. They sat at the council table, and the point was made that it was in this room and at this table that the decision to accept or reject their work would be made. We went around the table so that each new member could talk about their own vision for London, why they wanted to serve, and what problems they saw in London. We had comments such as, "I want to help build a city where my kids don't want to move away." Powerful. Magic started to happen that day, and it continued throughout the life of the task force.

We met every two weeks for six months, generally in two-hour sessions, and then a couple of more times to edit the report. We sat on the floor one night, eating pizza, and talking about "big dreams and big ideas" for London. We went out to bars and clubs on Friday night because we knew college and university students wouldn't come down to city hall to talk to us. We had a community open house on a blizzardy Saturday morning that featured live music, art, and cultural diversity in the city, and attracted an astonishing 65 people to talk about their vision for London. We reached out to young leaders, and did a road show at a heritage hall in a part of town that, at that time, wasn't necessarily leading-edge.

The London report was holistic in nature. The task force studied everything, including the way culture was handled inside the city. It was handled badly, as it turned out – scattered, unfocused, and with few resources. So, one of our key recommendations was to create a new culture office inside the CAO's department, consolidating the functions and increasing funding. In other words, "one-stop shopping" for the broad range of cultural activities and support. It is working beautifully.

There is a subtle but important difference in the type of report that may result. One approach is to focus more intently on economic development and culture, as well as to analyze other key segments, such as planning, the environment, city hall departments, etc. Another approach is to focus more on creative industries, arts, heritage, cultural activities, community resources, etc. – but without full integration into other areas of municipal planning. Both approaches can be effective – it simply depends on the needs of the community at that time.

There is no single "right or wrong" template for developing a Cultural Plan – the process and outcomes must always be shaped and tailored for the needs of that community. It is one of the great strengths of the "Creative City" process.

The London task force took just eight months from the first meeting to presentation of the report and recommendations to council. It was an astonishing commitment and effort from task force members. The process worked. The report has been applauded across Canada and used by other cities in North America as a template.

How your community does its plan is entirely up to you. Often, it will take longer, and that doesn't matter – what does matter is the quality of the research, the depth of the report, and the creativity of the recommendations.

That raises the question: Do we hire a consultant – and how much is this going to cost?

4. Consultants – Yes or No?

Engaging the community in the process is critically important. Much of the success from strong Cultural Planning comes from involving the community from the very start, and reaching out to engage the community. Don't stay cloistered behind the walls of your city hall – get out into the community, reach out to students who probably wouldn't come in to give you their ideas, learn about what's important to young leaders, visit downtown clubs and bars to get a sense of what entertainment there is, and what these people really think about your community.

Meet industry and manufacturing managers and leaders to find out what their issues are. Engage the colleges, universities, and schools, because they are leading the knowledge-based economy and can be huge supporters of efforts to become a Creative Community.

Get the arts, heritage, and cultural communities excited about the opportunities the process can offer them. If they are reluctant or negative, or start to get protective, ask them one simple question: "When was the last time the cultural agenda was before municipal council?"

Get the business community involved. Cultural Planning is about fundamental issues that confront leading companies today, and their input is invaluable. They will help to identify key questions in future job growth, and can provide answers. Should your community start a co-op program with university students? The University of Waterloo has become renowned for its co-op programs, and for the computer training the university offers, and is now a favourite recruiting spot for Bill Gates.

New technology. Innovation. Great jobs for bright young grads. These kinds of linkages can change a community. Waterloo, Ontario, meet RIM. World, meet the new Waterloo.

Whether you hire a consultant or not, you must – repeat, *must* – have an extensive community outreach as part of your Cultural Planning process.

A consultant can provide you with professional guidance in the process. She/he has experience and knowledge to offer, and can provide a calm outside viewpoint when internal disputes sometimes erupt. Having an independent moderator may be useful in the community participation process.

A good consulting firm – and there are some top-notch ones in Canada – experienced in Cultural Planning can offer very good value as part of your process.

One of the major considerations is: Who will write the final report? Writing is a skill that is not shared by everyone, yet is crucial to having a successful final result. If not a consultant, then who will do the writing and editing?

Who is going to keep track of the ideas and suggestions that come from the public consultations? Who is going to help form the task force's ideas into recommendations? Who will help with the research and documentation necessary to set the foundation for the final report? And, who will shape the final document? Consultants can certainly provide qualified help and direction in these areas.

A task force will generally need support from the municipal clerk's office. It will also need the support of senior staff who can offer expertise, experience, and thoughts for the future.

And, sometimes, the task force members themselves will decide to really make it their report by writing and editing their final report themselves. (This is most admirable, but be warned: writing a comprehensive report is a long, tough job. And, there's nothing like having a dozen well-meaning editors to help!)

Writing the report takes hard work, time, and effort. The task force must decide at an early stage what role it wishes to play, and what process it intends to follow.

If retaining a consultant for what will likely be a year-long process, expect to pay +/- $50,000 for a solid report. For a major report for a larger community, the price would rise. It could decrease a bit for smaller centres. Negotiation will be needed to clearly identify the responsibilities and roles of the consultant, time frames, travel and other expenses, the final report and printing, and other task force needs.

You will want to sign a letter of agreement with the consultant that spells out clearly the duties and responsibilities of each party, payment terms, and other conditions. And, the needs of communities for consulting services may vary considerably, from having the consultant lead the process in an independent manner, to having the consultant write the report, to having a consultant provide only general guidance to the task force, and then leaving it up to the task force members to do most of the work.

There is no right or wrong answer on hiring a consultant. It will depend upon a community's needs, the commitment and abilities of the collective task force members, and the process the community wishes to follow.

5. Framing the Work

Some useful early-stage work by the task force will help to frame the work and the eventual report. This involves identifying the major issues to be considered, and the large topics to be undertaken in the final report. These issues will vary from community to community, but there will be a number of consistent topics, such as:

► economic development and opportunities;

► downtown revitalization;

► development partnerships and private-public partnerships;

► Cultural Mapping;

► council's strategic planning and priorities;

► arts, culture, and heritage – strengthening the sectors;

► city hall issues – planning, engineering, parks, and recreation;

► environmental issues and opportunities;

► community revitalization, social issues, civic challenges; and

► unique local issues.

The task force may wish to focus on one of these major topics at a meeting, and then move on. The final report may utilize each of these major themes as a chapter and series of recommendations. This kind of process also "completes the circle" with the community – getting community input early in the process, then dealing with the identified major themes in the report, and offering recommendations to resolve or move ahead with the challenges and opportunities.

The task force will also need to understand that, sometimes, unanimity on an issue is just not possible. Sometimes, task force members will have a particular issue or strongly-held view that may be different from the majority of the members. Don't let this situation detract from the report. At the end of the day, the decision-making process of the task force must be open and positive, but it must also conclude with strong recommendations. The process can't be hijacked by any member of the task force.

Regardless of the process, it is important for the task force to deal honestly and openly with community issues. This is not an easy process. To undertake an effective Cultural Planning process, a community must have the courage to confront its challenges. The final report must be unblinking in its honesty. Most in the community will respect that determination by the task force to identify and then resolve lingering issues, and to provide a positive path for future growth and prosperity.

In other words, take a clear snapshot of the municipality today, and then present that in the final report. Don't hide problems, don't exaggerate the difficulties, and don't turn away from the blemishes in the community. All communities have them in some form. Then, once the community understands the problems, turn to the solutions. That will be the ultimate focus of the report – the vision, ideas, and positive recommendations.

Community members should have ample opportunity to address, discuss, present, and proffer their concerns, ideas, issues, challenges, fears, applause, and other emotions in an open and non-confrontational manner. Whether in public hearings by the task force, through emails and written presentations, through on-the-street discussions, through the task force going out into the community, or through roundtables and focus groups, it is important for the task force to be open, and to be seen to be open, to community input.

Engaging the public in the early stages of the process will pay huge dividends later. Encouraging public participation is a key element. This helps to frame the task force's work, the subsequent report and recommendations, and sends a clear message to the community that this is their report – not just another municipal document to be buried.

Happily, experience has shown that the public will always offer many bold, creative, and useable ideas and solutions. Nothing will complete the circle more than some community group or individual recognizing their issue or idea in the final report!

What else can a consultant do? Well, one of the first steps many communities choose to undertake in their research is Cultural Mapping to identify cultural resources and assets in their community – the subject of the next chapter.

In the chapters that follow next, we'll examine the various facets of community life that you'll want to explore in the development of your Cultural Plan, from economic development through to social, environmental and community challenges.

It is this holistic view of Municipal Cultural Planning that we present in this book. Developing a Creative Community involves many facets of municipal life. Integrating the various community parts into a stronger, more compelling whole is one of the great benefits of researching and implanting a community Cultural Plan.

That's why we have included sections on everything from public art to protecting heritage properties, from downtown redevelopment to building new neighbourhoods, from environmental protection to technological infrastructure. It is this total package, the complete picture, that separates your Cultural Plan from the typical municipal study and report that focuses on only one aspect of a community's development. In other words, usually a report on economic development, for one example, won't think about the impact of design of new bridges or infrastructure projects as public art opportunities.

Such reports *should* consider these factors, because all of these things combine to form a more creative, vibrant, and appealing community. That is the strength and the surprise to many of your Cultural Plan.

Chapter 4

Cultural Mapping

By Greg Baeker

Cultural Mapping is a process for systematically identifying a community's cultural assets and for deepening understanding of local cultural systems. There are two kinds of Cultural Mapping.

Resource mapping – identifying and documenting physical (or tangible) cultural resources;

Identity mapping – exploring and recording "intangible cultural resources" – the stories defining a community's unique identity and sense of place. (Groger, Mercer and Engwicht, 1995.)

Most of this chapter will address the first, cultural resource mapping.

Municipal Cultural Planning

Cultural Mapping is an integral part of a larger planning framework known as Municipal Cultural Planning (MCP), defined as:

> The strategic and integrated planning and use of cultural resources in economic and community development. (Municipal Cultural Planning Partnership.)

MCP has five defining characteristics that anchor the planning methodology.

1. Cultural resources – MCP embraces a broad definition of cultural resources that includes creative industries, cultural spaces and facilities, natural and cultural heritage, programs and activities.

2. Cultural Mapping – MCP is built on a systematic approach to identifying and recording cultural resources (using geographic information systems). Cultural mapping also examines the more intangible matter of a community's identity and sense of place.

3. New municipal roles – MCP calls on municipalities to play stronger strategic leadership roles in integrating culture across departments, internally and externally building strategic partnerships and sectoral capacity.

4. Cross-sectoral strategies – MCP requires effective ongoing collaboration with community and business partners and concrete mechanisms (such as roundtables) to support and sustain collaboration.

5. Networks and community engagement – MCP requires systematic approaches to ongoing engagement of the community and strengthening networks inside and outside the cultural sector.

Defining Cultural Resources

Michael Jones, a musician and leadership specialist, puts the need for new perspectives and new approaches to culture this way: "We're creating a new vocabulary. The boundaries of our language are the boundaries of our world. We need new words that conjure up something in our imaginations. We can't get there from here with the old language."

At the heart of Municipal Cultural Planning is the term "cultural resources." The value and power of the idea is that it starts the discussion not from the perspective of any one discipline or form of expression (visual arts, performing arts, museums, libraries, etc.), but from a larger overarching idea. The term also communicates an unapologetic view of culture as a resource for economic and broader community and human development.

A significant barrier to shifting the paradigm about culture in municipalities is the phrase "the arts and culture." The term is a relatively new one. When I worked at the Ontario Ministry of Culture in the late 1980s, there was never talk of "the arts and culture." Ministry policy addressed the arts, and it addressed culture, but they were not combined. If the focus was culture, it was understood to include policy related to the full spectrum of arts, heritage, libraries, and cultural (now creative) industries.

To talk about "the arts and culture" is like talking about "cardiology and medicine" or "baseball and sport." The arts are a critically important dimension of culture, but they cannot be confused with the larger phenomenon. Confusing the part with the whole paradoxically ensures the marginalization of both.

One of the traps in cultural policy, historically, has been defining culture either too broadly ("the unique ways of life that characterize a community or social group") or too narrowly (as in "the arts" or "the arts and heritage"). The concept of cultural resources establishes a useful middle ground. It embraces a broad definition of cultural assets or phenomenon, while still establishing limits or boundaries on the "object" of planning.

Cultural Resource Framework

A frequent misconception is that municipalities lack information on local cultural resources. The opposite is true. The problem is that this information is collected in different ways, by different people, for different purposes. The task is to consolidate information in coherent ways that support planning and decision making in cultural development. This requires building consensus among community partners on a Cultural Resource Framework (CRF) – a consistent categorization (typology) of cultural resources described in the previous section.

Broad categories of resources captured by the CRF are illustrated below. Each category is broken down into further sub-categories or disciplines.

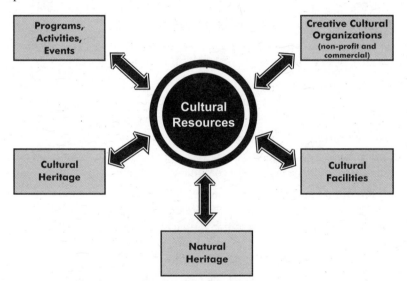

These categories reflect, to the greatest degree possible, the ways in which municipalities or key community partners already collect information. Naturally, this begins with the categories of creative cultural resources used by Statistics Canada (North American Standard Industrial Categories – NAICS.). It continues with categories of natural and cultural heritage defined by key provincial legislation that governs planning and policy making in municipalities. For example, in Ontario, the CRF reflects categories of natural and cultural heritage found in the

Ontario *Planning Act* and *Ontario Heritage Act*; and categories of attractions found in the Ministry of Tourism's Premier-ranked Tourism Destinations Framework.

The goal is to create a more consistent definition of cultural resources for purposes of provincial policy and legislation that integrates culture as part of (provincially mandated) municipal planning systems.

Initial Mapping Outcomes

There are four outcomes sought in a first phase of Cultural Mapping undertaken as part of completing a Municipal Cultural Plan.

1. Baseline map– *a comprehensive baseline of information on cultural resources entered into municipal GIS platforms and protocols.*

2. Partnership model – an agreement and set of commitments between the municipality and the community and business partners it will work with to maintain and expand the system over time. Mapping systems are not sustainable without such partnerships.

3. Technical protocols – clearly defined technical standards and protocols that ensure compatibility of information with municipal GIS.

4. Long range mapping plan – a longer-term plan for expanding Cultural Mapping consistent with the goals of the final Municipal Cultural Plan.

Uses of Cultural Mapping

Cultural mapping has three broad uses or applications in support of cultural development and creative community building.

1. Planning and policy – Mapping creates an up-to-date database to support evidence-based planning and decision making by municipalities. It can also serve as a resource for the municipality's business and community partners and, in so doing, support better informed and more collaborative planning with the community.

2. Marketing and promotion – Mapping results can be used to promote awareness of and participation in cultural activities by both residents and visitors. For example: a consistently updated calendar of cultural events and programs; themed tourism itineraries built around stories and narratives gathered through identity mapping; etc.

3. Access and cultural participation – Mapping can enhance access to the actual "content" of culture in the community. Web-based maps (i.e. e-maps) can serve as a dynamic point of access to cultural resources for the public, allowing points on a map to be linked to anything from descriptive blurbs and photographs, to web-links or podcasts, all of which can be explored using a search engine.

A Case Study

If all of this seems quite abstract, an example of how Cultural Mapping was implemented in one Canadian municipality may help. The Town of Oakville set out to develop a Municipal Cultural Plan in 2007. A staff steering committee representing 10 municipal departments and agencies oversaw the process – Culture and Recreation, Planning, Economic Development, Oakville Public Library, Oakville Centre for the Performing Arts, etc. A smaller mapping working group was struck to support Cultural Mapping.

The working group assessed a range of different sources of cultural information in the town. Three primary sources of data were chosen:

1. Your Local Marketplace – a business directory service subscribed to by the economic development office that had strong information on the "commercial" side of creative cultural industries.

2. Information Oakville – the community information centre in Oakville, an agency closely tied to the Oakville Public Library, which was a strong source of more community-oriented information.

3. Heritage data – information on natural and cultural heritage sites already in the planning department's databases.

The above data was consolidated into a single database. There was a certain amount of cleaning of the data – for example, removing duplicates. This data was then imported to the town's GIS system by the planning department.

Mapping Community Identity

Stories have been called the "DNA of culture." Cultural Mapping in any community is not complete without attention being paid to the "intangible" culture that collectively defines a community's unique identity and sense of place. Identity mapping can involve the following four steps.

1. Community-wide survey – A web-based survey tool (such as SurveyMonkey) can be used to distribute the identity mapping survey broadly across the community. This can be done through the networks and email lists of the municipality and its partners (eg. local arts councils, library members, BIA memberships, community foundations, etc.)

2. Identity mapping question – The survey invites people to think about the things that, for them, make their community unique – the im-

33

ages, places, stories, and qualities of place that define the community's identity and sense of place. It is also often useful to ask people to think ahead, to imagine their community as a prosperous, sustainable community in 20 years, and to describe that place. Questions can be a combination of open and closed (pre-determined choices) questions.

3. Synthesize themes and narratives – Responses are then collected and reviewed to identify overarching or recurring themes and narratives. The danger is boiling themes down so much that they become hollow and overly generalized. It is often useful to retain a writer or historian who can shape these themes into a compelling and powerful story that speaks to community and place identity.

4. Forums or focus groups – Depending on the project and available resources, these themes can be examined in more depth with various groups in the community. For example, they could be used to stimulate community dialogue and engagement in specific neighbourhoods, by school groups, by First Nations where they form a significant part of the population of that community, etc.

There is no expectation that the identity mapping conducted as part of a Municipal Cultural Plan is final or definitive. Quite the contrary, it is intended to begin a conversation in the community that stimulates residents to be more reflective and aware of place and identity.

[Note from Gord Hume:

These conversations that Greg talks about in his last paragraph can take many forms, and happen in many forums. We have included four fascinating case studies in Chapter 14, which offer detailed examples of the process and outcomes in four quite different Canadian communities. It is essential to understand the methodology and parameters, and why it is both useful and important to follow them. We have tried to be explicit in this book about "how to" so that communities have a focal point to begin.

It is equally important, however, that the outcomes and conclusions are specific for your municipality. This is a completely local process resulting in a completely unique result for every community – no two cultural reports will ever be the same. That is the great benefit, and the great secret, of Municipal Cultural Plans.

Both the resource and the identity mapping that Greg has talked about are basic components for many Cultural Plans. The following chapters provide further critical steps and advice.]

Chapter 5

Economic Development

Toronto Mayor David Miller was very clear in 2007: "We must put creativity at the heart of Toronto's economic development strategy."

It was that strong, ringing, and unequivocal call to action that spurred the 2008 report for Toronto city council: "Creative City Planning Framework – a supporting document to the agenda for prosperity."

That report makes a compelling case for the next wave of investment and support for Toronto's economic development through creativity. But, the report is also a call to action to make significant changes in planning and governance, cutting through administrative silos, realigning public and private sector agendas and resources, and revising a planning system so that it builds capacity as much as it sets direction.

It is a courageous and forward-thinking document that shows the clear links between a strong, prosperous city competing in a global economy today, and the foundational need for creativity throughout the municipal process.

This kind of thinking needs to occur in every Canadian community that wants to prosper in the future, create good jobs for its citizens, and enjoy a pleasant, healthy quality of life.

Cultural Planning for a Creative Community can help to drive this new thinking and way of doing business in the municipality.

Municipalities have always led change. As the level of government closest to the people, they are usually the first to hear about and respond to issues that are bubbling up in the community.

The pace of change in society has been speeding up. Just think about the advances in computers and technology. It wasn't all that many years ago that fax machines were introduced – wow, what a marvel then. Thirty years later, computers in police cars can get instant pictures and records of a suspect through a national crime database.

Traditional manufacturing jobs are being lost, many to overseas plants that operate at a much lower cost. But, new manufacturing jobs are being created in Canadian municipalities, and these jobs are high-tech at immaculate plants that feature everything from robotics to innovative scientific discoveries. Have no doubt – manufacturing today is very high-tech and very sophisticated. It is part of the CRINK economy.

As a society, we have evolved over the centuries from hunter-gatherers to an agrarian society to the industrial age, and now we are into the knowledge economy. Today, Canada's towns and cities are leading the creative-innovation-knowledge (the CRINK Economy) evolution because they realize that those are the jobs of the future. Innovation and creativity can flourish in any size community. Size and location are no deterrents for CRINK communities.

There are several mega-economic theories out there in the world, ranging from Thomas Friedman's *The World Is Flat*, which argues that, because of the Internet and technology, people and businesses in India, for example, can compete with the United States; to Richard Florida's *Who's Your City,* which postulates that the future economic powerhouses will be centred in a few mega-regions around the world, such as greater Tokyo ($2.5 trillion in economic output), the New York-Boston-Washington triangle ($2.2 trillion), and a few others.

All very interesting, but for a local town councillor who is fighting to keep a dozen jobs from leaving town and a small business from closing, global economic theories aren't very important at that moment.

Or, maybe they are.

Municipal politicians and administrators are pretty smart people. They have to deal with complex and multi-faceted issues on a regular basis. The topics change from aisle to aisle in the grocery store on a Saturday morning, as the councillor shops; the people asking the questions are the ones who do the voting and pay the taxes for all levels of government.

That is why really good municipal leaders do care about global economic theory. They have the capacity to bring it down to the local level and to understand why and how it is going to impact their community and neighbourhood. They also care about changing and shaping their community, be it large or small, to protect it from, adapt to, or grow with, a rapidly changing world economic climate.

When a Korean company invests in southern Ontario, there are global forces at work. When a Japanese corporation invests tens of millions of dollars in a small community like Woodstock, Ontario, it is changing that town. When European fishing fleets arrive on the Grand Banks, economic opportunity and crisis are both at play for Maritime villages. When China wants to buy oil companies exploring in Alberta and Saskatchewan, the new global economic realities are clear.

When oil prices spiked in 2008, municipal budgets were stressed because of higher fuel costs for transit fleets, police vehicles, and the entire municipal fleet. In the fall of 2008, when stock markets around the world crashed and credit markets snapped shut, even sturdy Canadian municipalities were vulnerable to the reduced availability of debentures for their community's capital needs.

Municipalities simply can't ignore global economic patterns. Like it or not, Canadian communities are now players in the world economy. That's why clever towns and cities are participating in international trade missions, working with the provincial and federal government liaison offices to seek new economic opportunities, and quietly changing their communities to adapt and welcome this new economic reality by making their town or city as progressive as possible. When Toronto and Beijing signed a "Culture of Partnership" in 2008 to provide greater opportunities between the cities, it sent a powerful message.

There is competition for economic growth and investment. Companies looking to expand or build in new markets have lots of choices. Many locations come with financial incentives from the local government, although Canadian municipalities are generally restricted in what they can offer. American cities are not constrained the same way.

Municipalities are also constrained in their ability to directly impact industry. Municipalities are not at the table for international trade discussions, have no role in setting tariffs or import quotas, can't set corporate tax levels, and so on. But, pursuing advantages locally through Cultural Planning and make a vibrant Creative Community is something that local government can achieve.

As a result, Canadian municipalities must offer a superior quality of life, access to a highly skilled labour force, a more appealing lifestyle for the employees, a safer community, a comfortable family environment, and the other elements that make up the kind of communities we have in Canada.

That is also why it is so important for municipalities in this country to utilize the tools and skills required for a strong local economy, such as Cultural Planning. And, as has been proven, having a vibrant and attractive community is one of the things that separate Canadian munici-palities from many others around the world. That ranges from a good library system, to arts and cultural opportunities, to providing safe wa-ter. What a municipality does, in fact, makes a difference.

The fundamental question is shifting today from the traditional "build it and they will come," to the newer "good business will follow good people." In other words, CRINK businesses will be attracted to com-munities where bright young people congregate, where innovation is encouraged, where the quality of life is appealing, where downtowns are buzzing, where technology is leading-edge, and where there is a constant demand by leading municipalities to pursue an agenda of innovation and excellence.

Lots of good jobs are going to be created in such a community. Compa-nies will start. Plants will expand. The municipal assessment base will grow.

One of the many benefits of this kind of progressive economic develop-ment policy is that clusters of innovation are encouraged.

Clusters can happen from similar businesses being grouped in the same general area (fast food restaurants have known for decades the benefits of being together, and car dealers are increasingly working together on large automotive malls or districts), or from clusters of talented people. In other words, it is minds generating innovative ideas, feeding off each other, that lead to business, scientific, or technological innovation.

Another courageous opportunity for local economic development cor-porations is to offer facilities and incubators that encourage the devel-opment of these clusters. If you look at San Jose or Waterloo, for exam-ple, they have been very successful in setting up incubator facilities that further the success of new anticipated industries. Kitchener, Ontario has recently announced its commitment to a new $500,000 digital me-dia incubator. By putting this cornerstone in place, it can generate sub-stantial returns; however, the municipality must focus on a specific area.

Technology transfer is one of the most sought-after benefits for a mu-nicipality fortunate enough to have a university, college, health care, re-search institution, or innovative private business that is a leader in sci-ence, medicine, engineering, research, innovation, and development. In other words, how does that idea get into the market place? How does it translate into high-paying jobs and benefit the local economy?

That is what local economic development corporations (be they private-sector driven or a civic department) can help to accomplish. Smart economic development professionals realize that the CRINK economy offers enormous economic benefit to their municipalities today.

Start-up companies can be huge economic generators, and can create new jobs for other members of the Creative Class. That is how regions like the Silicon Valley, Austin, Boston, and the Tech Triangle in North Carolina became so progressive.

Municipal economies that depend primarily on one traditional industry are more vulnerable to economic stress and downturns. Municipalities that have a diversified economic base and an emphasis on research, development, innovation, and tech transfer are in a vastly stronger economic position.

It is this hard-nosed business reality that is driving municipalities to change how they have traditionally done business. A strong local economy means a prosperous municipality, better able to serve its constituents in all socio-economic levels, to provide a high quality of life, and to compete positively in the global economy.

And, it is this need for a more global view that progressive councils must offer. The Creative Class hold a lot of the cards – their creativity, their degrees, their research, their innovation, their brains. They offer those resources to companies located in municipalities where life is fun and exciting. Borders don't mean much to them. They can do their scientific and medical research in New Zealand as easily as New York; they can cut high quality audio tracks in London, England or London, Ontario; they can produce world-class video and graphic game designs in Edmonton or Hong Kong.

The links between this fundamental economic reality for communities in the 21st century meet squarely with the Cultural Planning that progressive municipalities are doing today.

Judith Maxwell is the well-respected former head of the Economic Council of Canada. In a thoughtful article in the June 16, 2008 edition of *The Globe and Mail*, she commented, "So, where do governments come in? First, they can be the champions for the new ideas the networks generate, and for the networks themselves – what author Richard Florida would call the new Creative Class." Then, she concluded, "Ideas are now the essential raw material for growth and productivity. Informal networks are the 21st century blast furnace, where the raw ideas are formed and developed into products and processes that will drive the high growth businesses in our future."

Many small businesses and creative industries identify human capital as their primary asset. That also means those assets are highly mobile and their departure can leave a gaping hole in a local economy. You want these industries and businesses in your community, and your Cultural Plan can help guide your municipality's economic development efforts as well.

Most of the good jobs of the future are going to be in the CRINK economy. That is a simple reality. Knowing that, surely it makes sense for Canada's towns and cities to prepare now to make their community as appealing as possible to the Creative Class, to attract interesting new companies that feature innovation, technology and creativity, and to build their municipality for the future. It just makes good economic sense.

The following are some foundational issues to consider in your Cultural Planning process as you examine your community's economic structure, opportunities, and future growth.

1. Analyzing Your Municipality's Economic Base

What are the strengths of your local economy? What makes it vulnerable to downturns? How is it changing? What can the municipality do to help? What will the local economy be like in 10 years? What must our community do to thrive in the global marketplace? What are the jobs of the future?

These are fundamental questions for a community, and they will likely form part of your Cultural Planning analysis and report.

This is also a critical time to get the local business community, economic development partnership, university/college president, and other key players ranging from labour leaders to manufacturing general managers, from housing and development companies to emerging leaders, involved with your Cultural Planning process.

Creative companies and industries are already a large part of your community's economic base. The creative industries bring the human capital to develop, expand, enhance, and grow the local economic base. A strong, forward-thinking Cultural Plan provides fresh direction and energy to the local municipality.

2. Demographic Trends

The population of Canada is aging – is your community? Are young people leaving after they graduate to go to larger centres? Will seniors demand a greater share of your municipal resources in the future? What will that mean to traditional municipal thinking and budgeting, on everything from recreation programs to housing?

A key concern for North American communities is the growing population of seniors and the diminishing number of young workers. This has fundamental questions for the kind of local government priorities that will occur in the future. If your community can't attract and retain enough young workers, the demographic realities will force huge changes on local government. The municipal economic base will be threatened.

The trend can also provide an opportunity, if the municipality can attract seniors in search of a strong support network. For example, Elliott Lake, Ontario advertises low-cost housing and an attractive lifestyle for seniors. If the municipality provides amenities and attractions for these active, involved seniors who enhance a community, then new economic and social opportunities are being created.

At the other end of the scale, providing cultural infrastructure for the Creative Class also offers substantial benefits – for example, an appropriate concert hall/live entertainment facility that will attract concerts and events for this younger generation. Without these kinds of facilities, municipalities will have much more difficulty keeping the talent in their communities. In other words, cultural facilities and activities play an important role in attracting/retaining younger workers, the Creative Class, and emerging leaders. Having good entertainment venues, an active club and restaurant scene, and lots of "buzz" around town all add to the attractiveness of your community.

3. Societal Changes

The collapsing stock markets in 2008, the spike in oil prices followed by dramatic declines, and the shocking vulnerability of international financial markets and traditional manufacturing industries have shaken global economies. Volatility and uncertainty are the harsh realities for a while, and that will impact government spending and strategic planning. The development of strong, diverse local economies and the building of Creative Communities are emerging opportunities.

There are some who believe that this new economic climate will mean economic opportunity for small- and mid-sized cities. These communities offer lower housing prices, shorter commutes, arguably a better quality of life for families, and other pleasant surprises. With electronic and technological advances, companies no longer need to be downtown in some urban environment to do business.

Governments at all levels are often slow to respond to these tectonic shifts in our society. A municipality alert for new economic development opportunities, and armed with a strong economic strategy and Cultural Plan, offers increasing appeal to many workers and companies.

A Cultural Plan can help to identify these trends and opportunities, and set the framework and parameters for communities of all sizes to prosper. For example, the very recent trend of "near shoring" (buying more locally/regionally) positions Canada well.

4. Immigration and Foreign Investment

It is abundantly clear now that Canada will not produce enough employees for its future needs. The population is aging, skilled trades people in many sectors are retiring, and there is a growing demand for many types of employees in both traditional and new businesses.

We need immigration to fill this growing demand for skilled trades. Yet, traditionally, about 75 percent of immigrants to Canada end up in Montreal, Toronto, or Vancouver. And foreign investment dollars tend to follow those patterns.

How are the rest of Canada's cities and towns going to attract immigrants? A strong Cultural Plan can offer insight and direction. For example:

▶ by creating a web portal that offers "one-stop shopping" for potential immigrants;

▶ by encouraging clusters of immigrants to arrive;

▶ by municipalities being respectful of and sensitive to the art, cultural, family, faith, and food requirements of newcomers.

As the dispersal of different groups occurs, it is the communities in which they live that will shape the kinds of citizens they will become, and the kind of contributors they will be to the local economy and culture.

Is there a place to buy groceries and food stuffs that are familiar to immigrants? Is there a place for them worship? Does the community provide English as a second language or adult literacy programs? Will foreign professional credentials be recognized? Does the municipality provide a welcoming introduction to local arts and culture? How do you help them understand that the police in Canada are not corrupt and don't torture people? How do they link with other families from their region who have immigrated previously?

These are fundamental issues today that a creative, progressive Canadian community must face.

Federal and provincial governments are often too remote to get down to the realities of life for these immigrants, and how they will be welcomed, absorbed, and respected in their new home towns. Municipal governments and local support agencies are going to be the front-line of this new dynamic.

Smaller towns and cities may have to lobby hard with senior governments to see a second wave of migration of immigrants to small- and mid-sized communities. Immigration must be seen by municipalities as their responsibility, too. Where clusters of immigrants locate, often foreign investment will follow, creating a new economic base for that municipality.

5. Technological Infrastructure

In what shape is your community's technology infrastructure? Do you have the high-speed wiring in place to handle the demands of creative companies today, and in the future? Is WI-FI available downtown? Is it free?

What kind of computer facilities and services does your library system offer? Roughly a quarter of Canadians still don't have a home computer ... your municipality can't afford to have a community of information haves and have-nots.

If you don't have these kinds of services up and running, how will your community attract high-tech companies? Biotechnology, research, and medicine are all dependent upon reliable, high quality, and available technological infrastructure. But, so are video game designers, publishers, marketing businesses, and other CRINK industries.

6. Traditional Infrastructure

With a municipal infrastructure deficit in Canada today that has soared past the $100 billion mark, there is a national crisis. Yet, senior governments seem eerily unaware, or offer only tepid assistance to what has become a disgrace. Nation-building seems to be forgotten and national projects and passions have dropped off their radar screens.

It is left to municipalities to struggle against the growing burden of hundred-year-old sewer and water pipes bursting, potholes on major traffic arteries, a hydro system that cannot always provide low-cost, reliable, and high quality power to businesses that depend upon it, and the other parts of the local infrastructure system that are breaking.

Companies and foreign investors expect a certain level of competency and quality before they drop millions of dollars into a local economy. That is why infrastructure issues, both traditional and technological, are part of the considerations in developing a Creative Community. A municipality needs that core competency to attract the Creative Class and the companies of the future.

7. Cultural Infrastructure

There is a growing realization that we also have a significant cultural infrastructure deficit in Canada. Arts and culture have traditionally been underfunded by all levels of government, yet these industries represent about eight percent of our country's GDP.

This doesn't mean a new performing arts centre in every community; it does mean appropriate funding for an economic driver that creates jobs, investment, economic benefit, and export opportunities.

Establishing arts districts can be an exciting method of rejuvenating a stagnant area of a city. Around the world, artists and artisans are leading urban redevelopment – from New York, to Beijing's 798 district, to Paducah, Kentucky, to Shanghai's M50 arts district – the arts are often the first step in a neighbourhood's rebirth.

8. Small and Medium Enterprises (SMEs)

About 80 percent of all new jobs in Canada each year are created by small- and medium-sized businesses. They are crucial to any municipality's prosperity. Yet, too often, they are ignored by governments.

Local governments should take a critical look at their internal systems, approval process, information handling, communication, and inspection procedures to find efficiencies and ease of handling. SMEs simply don't have the time or resources to waste with municipal bureaucracy. And, because so many new SMEs are being started by the Creative Class, this can be a significant source of irritation and negativity in a municipality's relationship with its entrepreneurs.

A Cultural Plan Report can really help to shine some light on antiquated procedures and regulations. Members of the Creative Class aren't always as aware of or sensitive to by-law issues, zoning problems, inspections, and so on … they just want to get on with their business or art or creative enterprise. A municipality that can help to ease these conflicts will soon be getting a reputation amongst immigrants and the bright young Creative Class members as an appealing and welcoming place to do business. That word of mouth is invaluable in building a strong, diversified local economy.

9. Economic Diversity

Improving the economic diversity of a community is crucial. Cultural Planning can offer new opportunities. For example, tourism is a welcome part of the economic base, because tourists leave lots of cash in a community. Cultural Planning can help to identify new business opportunities.

Stratford, Ontario has a well-earned reputation for its Shakespearean festivals, and Niagara-on-the-Lake for its Shaw productions. Prince Edward County in eastern Ontario has done a brilliant job in developing a food/wine/tourism strategy that is now attracting large numbers of people. The wine tours of the Okanagan Valley in British Columbia, and the Niagara Peninsula in southern Ontario are high on "must visit" lists for many people.

In fact, food and wine are great opportunities for new economic development. Canada has unique and wonderful foods – salmon from the rivers of New Brunswick, Saskatoon berries, wild rice from Manitoba, tortieres and cheese from Quebec, fiddlehead greens from the Maritimes, maple syrup, ice wine, and so many more. Our chefs and our products are world-class.

Again, what opportunities are there for you? From the traditional and wonderful lobster suppers in Prince Edward Island and Nova Scotia to the marvelous cuisine of Quebec's historic culture, this is something for Canada to celebrate. And, it doesn't have to be big and complicated – think of the wonderful Butter Tart Trail that a dozen small towns in central Ontario put together. It is exactly what you think it is – wandering from bakery to farm, sampling different varieties of butter tarts and other local produce. Brilliant!

10. Municipal Leadership

A municipality can show real leadership to the business community and the Creative Class by starting, encouraging, or assisting a wide variety of programs and initiatives aimed at assisting graduates get jobs in their local community, instead of heading automatically for the nearest big city.

45

Coming out of university or college, students are focused on one thing and one thing only – getting a good job.

For a community to see these wonderfully bright young people leave and take their talents and economic contributions elsewhere is a tremendous loss. For a smaller town or rural area, the impact can be even more devastating.

There are some things progressive communities can do to appeal to and attract these valuable economic resources of graduating students and recent immigrants.

Some important ideas and examples are:

► Co-op job programs – working with the local college or university to link with the business community. Once students develop a relationship with a good local company, they are much more likely to consider staying in your community after graduation.

► Develop linkages with the students when they first arrive in your community, not the month before they graduate. Make sure these students understand about your downtown, the neighbourhoods, what the community has to offer, and reach out to them.

► Honour and respect the First Nations and immigrant communities through civic recognition and leadership.

► Support adult literacy programs (through local libraries and community resource centres).

► Encourage, at all levels of municipal government (from city hall to the police department), the hiring of a diverse workforce to reflect your diverse community.

► Work with the local labour council to support apprenticeship and work experience programs. The skilled trades are a hugely important part of every local economy, and we need more skilled trades people.

► Encourage local companies to participate in job fairs at colleges and schools.

► Offer mentorship programs between emerging leaders and established leaders in the business community, including managers at city hall.

► Provide summer work programs at municipal institutions, and work with the local chamber of commerce and other business groups to encourage students to stay in town for the summer.

▶ Work with professional associations and other quasi-agencies to ensure professional credentials and work experience from other countries are given fair consideration.

▶ Break down barriers between businesses and their need for skilled workers, and the new economy participants – immigrants, graduates, Creative Class members.

▶ Support job-shadowing programs to help provide valuable training and experience for immigrants and students. Your municipality has lots of such opportunities.

▶ Develop and support a climate of entrepreneurship in your community.

You will find and create other local ideas and opportunities; the list above is just a thought-starter for your Cultural Planning Report process.

11. Emerging Leaders

One of the greatest resources to a community of any size is the smart and creative young people who will become the future leaders.

Yet, many communities have ignored this marvelous resource, or have failed to take advantage of the youth, energy, enthusiasm, fresh ideas, and different approaches that these clever young women and men offer.

Generally, these emerging leaders are in their 20s or 30s, but sometimes even exceptional teens will want to get involved with their community. It is crucial for municipalities to nurture and support such attitudes.

These are also the people who will create much of the buzz about your community, and freely tell their compatriots about the goods and bads of life in your community. If they feel welcome, they are a huge plus for the community. If they are discouraged, they will likely leave town and say negative things about you for some time to come, creating an impression that will be extremely difficult to overcome.

Here are a few successful ideas to retain and support the Gen X and Yers:

▶ Get a support group started for the emerging leaders. One of the big obstacles for many of them starting out in businesses is simply the contacts they need to develop. Networking opportunities are a huge bonus for them. Once this group is started, it will flourish on its own.

▶ Save a seat at the boardroom table of your municipality's agencies, boards, and commissions for a young leader. Get them

47

serving. Get their energy on these boards. By involving them in the full decision making of municipal government, you start sinking their roots into your community.

▶ Develop a mentorship program involving your council members, senior staff, and business leaders. Involve these emerging leaders in municipal governance matters, as well as helping to hone their own research, analytical, and media skills.

▶ Create a local internship program involving post-secondary institutions + your municipality + local businesses + social agencies to develop strong bonds between local industry and the students – which can also open the door for summer work programs, and even full-time employment after graduation.

These are very savvy media and tech people; don't hesitate to give them some media exposure. They have grown up in a media world of video, blogs, cell phones, and cable news networks. In fact, they might even teach you a few things about media and new media opportunities.

Economic development and Cultural Planning may, at first, seem to be strange bedfellows. But, as this chapter has proven clearly, they are linked closely and inextricably. Municipalities that recognize this partnership have a tremendous competitive advantage.

Members of the Creative Class are not going to stay in or be attracted to communities that are dull, old-fashioned, boring, or inept. They won't go to communities that have dying downtowns. They won't stay in communities that are technological luddites. They won't start their businesses in a place where innovation and creativity are discouraged or mocked. They won't live in a community where they have no social stimulation. They won't stay in a community that is intolerant of different lifestyles and social relationships.

Knowing this, smart municipalities can grow in smart ways, and develop the Cultural Planning process. They can shape and re-shape their communities. They can provide the kind of physical, business, and social environments that are appealing. They can provide fun and healthy neighbourhoods and places to live.

The "Creative City" movement is about creating a vibrant, healthy community that has a strong, diversified base for economic prosperity.

Chapter 6

Downtown Revitalization and Heritage Properties

If there is a common thread that links municipalities of all sizes across Canada, it is surely the desire for a vibrant, strong, and economically robust downtown core.

Even highly successful municipalities have some streets or pockets of their downtown that have become less desirable. Many are, in fact, a blight on the municipality – dark, dirty, dangerous. Empty stores and buildings. Filth blowing around the streets. The sex and drug trades active. The stench of failed businesses.

Often, the situation must reach almost a crisis before the council's attention is really focused on positive solutions.

In many towns and cities, there is still a belief that a healthy downtown reflects a prosperous community. Many citizens, fairly or not, judge the overall economic health of the community based upon their perceptions of the downtown core.

Downtowns are important. They are the historic centre of the municipality, where the economic, social, and political history of the municipality collides. Often, the founding families still have ties to the community. Long-time merchants have served their communities for decades, arts and cultural centres have excited audiences for generations, and the political, legal, and community heart of the municipality is still likely based in the core.

With the rise of suburban living in the 50s and 60s, a new era was born in North American cities. Shopping malls arose, offering climate controlled experiences and free parking. More recently, discount centres and big box outlets have emerged in most communities.

Traditional shopping patterns have changed dramatically. Downtowns are never going to return to their retail glory days when families dressed up and went to gaze in awe at the Christmas displays in the department store windows. But, downtowns today are even more important in a Creative Community, because members of the Creative Class often want to live, work, and certainly play in a clean, dynamic, safe, and interesting downtown that has "buzz."

Successful downtowns today are being driven by four primary themes, all of which are key Cultural Planning goals:

1. Arts, Heritage, and Culture

Generally, downtowns are the home for the festivals, street performances, museums, art galleries, studios, public spaces, theatres, performing arts centres, libraries, public art, and the other components of a vibrant cultural scene. Downtowns are often the home for heritage properties, and there is a new respect for preserving and protecting these unique heritage structures.

2. Food and Fun

Clubs, bars, restaurants, hotels, dance studios, cafes, coffee shops, bistros, patios, street food, outdoor events ... people like having fun downtown, celebrating family and personal milestones, coming together for major events and community functions.

3. Business and Commerce

From office buildings to specialized retail operations that offer distinctive merchandise and services, there is a natural agglomeration in the core. Many people still go to work downtown every day; the question increasingly is, however, are they connecting with their downtown?

4. Residents

More and more people are living downtown. For some communities, this is a new phenomenon; for others (especially large cities), it is the trend of recent decades – build up, not out. You need a certain number of people living in a dense area to create a neighbourhood – at least 10,000 people is the generally accepted number. That creates the opportunity for retail services like a grocery store.

For a Creative Community, downtowns play a critical role. And, there is usually a considerable reservoir of public support for a healthy downtown. In fact, there is a strong argument to be made that the downtown is one of a community's economic spires – that the business activity generated in a downtown is just as important to many civic economies as the manufacturing sector, research and technology, and so on.

When a community adds up the employment, the commercial activity, the capital investments, and the tax base in its downtown, it is an impressive total.

For members of the Creative Class, downtowns are often both a residence and a workplace. In fact, they can be combined into what is known as live/work/play/display space – an art studio that has a living space at the rear and a gallery in the front, for example.

Students and young people are also keen to experience the night life their community offers, so clubs and bars are of particular interest to them. Many of these people don't own cars, so public transportation or living close to where they play is important.

They are looking for the "buzz" that comes from a vibrant, active, and exciting downtown. It is peer group pressure, it is social interaction, it is the fun and excitement of growing up – and a community that doesn't offer some buzz is going to be in trouble.

This is the same group that, the next morning after partying and socializing the night before, is going to head out to do groundbreaking research, or design the next big hit for video games, or develop a marketing campaign that blows the doors off a business, or create the next piece of sculpture that awes critics.

You want them in your community.

If you don't want them, they will leave quickly for more enlightened, interesting, and creative communities.

What makes up a robust, fun, and strong downtown today? Several elements. Downtowns must:

- ▶ be welcoming;
- ▶ be safe;
- ▶ be fun;
- ▶ celebrate the community's diversity;
- ▶ be green;
- ▶ offer unique experiences;
- ▶ be pedestrian-oriented;
- ▶ provide a sense of pride of place;
- ▶ celebrate a community's history and heritage;
- ▶ be attractive;

- ▶ offer public art, public spaces, and public experiences;

- ▶ be densely populated with bustling energy on the streets;

- ▶ be the creative heart of the community;

- ▶ be the social centre, where people of all strata and sectors can meet and interact in safety and security;

- ▶ be people-oriented, not just people-friendly;

- ▶ provide gathering places for public performances and events; and

- ▶ offer good signs and maps to tell people what is available and where.

Assessing what problems your downtown is facing can be daunting. It takes clear eyes and unblinking honesty, but the process is necessary if you're going to develop a viable redevelopment plan.

What is the physical construct of your downtown (or the area of concern in the downtown)? Are the streets and sidewalks narrow? Is there good lighting, from both the sun and from street lamps, or is the atmosphere dark? Is the streetscape physically attractive and appealing? Are there closed and darkened buildings? Is there life and energy on the street, or is it depressing and dangerous? Are there places for the public to gather? Is there public art that interests, even titillates? Is there street food offered, with patios and cafes, fountains or squares to attract people? Are the merchants busy? Are there trees and green spaces? Does your downtown provide a pleasurable experience for visitors? Are there special attractions to get office workers out of their hermetically-sealed buildings at noon hour? What kind of traffic and parking issues are there? Does public transportation provide safe, reliable, and timely service? Is visiting downtown fun?

Fundamental questions. Difficult answers.

Each community will find its own issues, challenges, and opportunities. Answers must be tailored for that town or city. The business association must be intimately involved. Council must be prepared to take action. And, the public must be supportive of what could be major change.

Generally, however, there are some common problems that must be confronted by the council:

Is city hall responsive to downtown issues?

Sometimes, developers are frustrated by what they perceive as stifling bureaucracy, overzealous regulations, and inflexible staff at their local municipal office. Often, a first step to successful downtown rejuvenation is having the council look hard at its internal operations, approval process, inspections, by-laws, and communication and information methods.

Are zoning by-laws and the official plan up to date?

Do the zoning by-laws encourage innovation downtown? Do they permit the live/work/play/display spaces to encourage arts and artisans, members of the Creative Class and young entrepreneurs to get started? Make sure your official plan reflects the kind of downtown you want to create.

Should incentive plans be available?

Can the municipality offer incentives to developers and landlords to improve their buildings? (For a detailed list of suggestions, see Chapter 8.)

Are tax policies progressive or detrimental?

Are the property taxes being assessed fairly? Are property taxes reasonable compared to other parts of the municipality? Are there incentives (sometimes because of provincial law) to allow landlords to keep buildings vacant and get a tax rebate, rather than encourage redevelopment? More importantly, does the public believe they are getting reasonable value for their taxes?

Has council provided modern infrastructure in the downtown?

Are there potholes and unsafe gaps in the streets and sidewalks? Are the water and sewer lines in good shape? Is there a reliable, secure, and high quality supply of hydro? You can never redevelop a downtown if the infrastructure is broken.

What is the technology infrastructure like?

Is the community wired with fibre optics? Is there free WI-FI downtown? Is the community connected, so that businesses and individuals can access the highest quality technology? These are fundamental necessities to attract CRINK industries such as scientific and medical research, software and graphic designers, financial institutions, data providers, marketing companies, and other contemporary businesses.

Is the downtown green?

Are there big, green, leafy trees growing? Is the downtown clean, or is it filthy with cigarette butts and waste blowing in the street? People are increasingly intolerant of communities that aren't demonstrably green and providing clear leadership for environmental issues.

Do people feel safe and comfortable in the core?

Is there a strong police presence? Is there attractive, clean street furniture for the public to enjoy? Are public washrooms available? People must have a great experience every time they visit your downtown, because there are too many options out there for them otherwise.

Who rules – vehicles or pedestrians?

Is the downtown people-oriented, or just people-friendly? Do cars have the right of way, or do pedestrians and shoppers? Does public transportation offer great service? A strong downtown needs feet on the street; that means bustling, exciting energy with lots of people having fun and doing business.

What is the role of public spaces and public art?

Are there interesting public spaces downtown? Plazas, squares, parks, or piazzas for people to gather, interact, share, relate. Is there public art to interest and excite, to provoke and amuse?

Are there enough people living in the area?

Is there a neighbourhood feel? Is there a diverse variety of people living there? Are there different options for housing offered, at different price ranges? Are there families living downtown? Is public housing available? Having a true neighbourhood feel to the core solves a lot of other issues. Most people instinctively protect each other and their property. Having lots of people downtown makes it a safer, more fun, and more interesting place to live.

These are some of the primary questions for which a municipality should take responsibility. They may be prodded by the public, the business improvement area board, downtown property owners, crusading local media, or a neighbourhood group seeing property values declining and safety issues arising.

Larry Beasley, the noted urban planner from Vancouver who has drawn worldwide attention with his innovative ideas and leadership, observes that a successful residential neighbourhood (and downtowns are a neighbourhood) needs three things – food, pharmacy, and liquor. In other words, easy access by the residents to certain comforts and needs. But, you need the critical mass of people available before you can interest a grocery chain in starting a store in the core.

Fixing a downtown is not, however, solely the responsibility of the local council. It must be a partnership between the community, businesses, social agencies, cultural organizations, media, and the public.

What is clear is that providing a vibrant core is important to the Creative Class, and that much of this "buzz" can be generated by effective, intelligent Cultural Planning from the municipal council.

Arts, culture, artisans, and the Creative Class are leading economic indicators for a strong community. There are clear correlations between a robust local economy and a vibrant, culturally-strong community. And, it all starts with the natural gathering place for people – a fun and exciting downtown.

That is why downtowns are important to a Creative Community.

Heritage Buildings

Many North American communities have seen a deterioration of buildings and properties in their downtowns. Typically, these areas are amongst the oldest of any community, and it is a simple equation: many decades, even a century, of wear and tear, being battered by weather and indifferent owners, often compounded by neglect and ignorance, results in sad, desolate buildings in disrepute and disrepair.

At the same time, however, the rich patina of lovingly restored heritage building adds character, style, and historic context to a neighbourhood – something that can't be repeated by another shiny glass tower.

This is why smart communities are turning their eyes to protecting and preserving heritage buildings in the core.

How can a municipality change the dark, empty space of closed, deteriorating buildings into vibrant new stores, artists' lofts, studios, and dining rooms?

First, understand that landlords and building owners are often long-time owners of the property, perhaps even second- or third-generation. They have seen boom and bust times in the downtown. They may be absentee property owners who have watched with dismay as downtown property values dropped.

They have not reinvested in their buildings, for many reasons:

► they can't get tenants who will pay to renovate their building and sign a long-term lease;

► they can't get a mortgage, or sometimes can only get a modest percentage of what they believe to be the value of the building from their bank or lending institution;

► to reopen or expand the building, they are confronted immediately with new provincial rules or municipal by-laws dealing with fire codes, building codes, accessibility upgrades, etc.;

► heritage properties being renovated often come with problems and expensive surprises and complications;

► the approval/inspection process is too long, too complicated, and too frustrating;

► if they reopen one floor of the building, what do they do with the rest of the building?

Costs are obviously a concern and a hindrance. Renovation costs are often very high and, as surprises are discovered, the price can jump. Landlords are very nervous about starting a potentially long, difficult, and expensive process. In fact, experience has shown that it is not unusual for renovation costs to equal or exceed the purchase price of downtown buildings.

Things to Consider

There are several key things for a municipality to consider – and the list of things possible will vary from province to province, depending on their laws and regulations.

Work with the downtown business improvement area – They are the "on the street" resources that today must do more than the traditional "beautify and promote" activities of decades past. They must be an aggressive partner, sometimes arbitrator, sometimes hand-holder, sometimes kick-in-the-pants, with downtown property owners and the municipality to resolve issues.

Have a cold, hard look at your downtown, its buildings, its challenges, and its future – In other words, get an honest report and a doable plan put together. Identify "at risk" buildings.

Development corporations (municipal) are still relatively rare in Canada, but they have been popular in the US for some time – The concept is simple: a combination of public and private sector money, energy, and resolve come together to identify buildings, districts, or neighbourhoods that need help. They fix up the building, rent it or sell it, buy another property, and the cycle continues. The benefit of an independently-run development corporation is that it can be more nimble and less political than a city hall committee.

Change the way you do business inside city hall – Review your approval and inspection processes. Assign a bright, young (both characteristics can be important!) manager to be the "good shepherd" for heritage buildings or special projects, to speed approvals, provide advice, and keep the files moving.

Get council approval for a variety of incentive programs aimed at special incentive zones, downtown blocks, or heritage properties – Some ideas are detailed in Chapter 8, Planning and Place-making Tools.

Seek opportunities to attract artists and the Creative Class to interesting historic buildings and districts – Having artists and the cultural community lead a downtown renaissance is a proven way of changing and improving that neighbourhood. They bring energy, fun, and business – and welcome buzz – to the street. From Beijing to New York, this is a successful business pattern.

Select specific buildings to be converted/renovated to become an Artists' Hub – These projects have been wildly successful in Edmonton, Toronto, and other cities. A building – often a heritage building – is renovated to allow live/work/play/display space for artists and artisans. Their creative energy feeds off one another, and the display and sales area in the building often becomes a significant attraction.

Develop a process to match existing landlords with prospective tenants – The young Creative Class is developing new and different retailing concepts today, many of which fit beautifully into heritage buildings – but are not following a traditional business plan. Guerilla marketing relies on text messages, word of mouth, and buzz for the short life of such projects – these stores may only be open for a few weeks or months. Alley and "nook and cranny" stores are tucked into laneways or rear access locations. Multi-purpose stores open with two or three compatible products, and don't carry other more traditional merchandise. In other words, tenants' needs today can be vastly different from even a decade ago, and many traditional landlords are behind the times.

Parking issues have tormented municipal leaders for decades – Cities often control perhaps only 20 percent of parking spaces in a core area, but get flogged by angry business owners, environmentalists, downtown advocates, and drivers for: not enough parking spaces; too many parking spaces; too expensive parking; too cheap parking; not enough long-term (i.e. monthly) parking; not enough short-term (i.e. street or parking lots) parking; and so on. Parking is pretty much a no-win issue for civic officials.

Transit is the hot item right now – Senior governments are pouring billions into public transit services through the gas tax payments to municipalities. Communities of all sizes are trying to provide increased public transit services, while balancing the well-established equation of increased fares resulting in lower ridership. Investing in public transportation infrastructure is appealing to all three orders of government. Better service and facilities will mean steadily increasing use of public transportation. This will also help local governments to shape their downtowns, suburban neighbourhoods, and future planning requirements.

Heritage Properties Can be an Asset – But Not Always

Heritage properties can be one of a community's greatest assets downtown – or in other residential neighbourhoods. These unique properties celebrate the architecture and design of a different century, and often reflect the building materials and contextual space that helped to build a particular community. These unique buildings can separate one community from another. They can offer specific answers to those who challenge a community's character and uniqueness, if nothing but endless rows of fast food joints, cheap strip malls, and big box stores dominate.

At the same time, however, a municipality shouldn't be held hostage to a deteriorating heritage building. Some landlords will deliberately wait for a building to decline dramatically, and then try to get a heritage designation, and then demand the municipality buy the building or it will fall into – well, a pile of rubble. Often, the local media and heritage activists get excited about this possibility, and suddenly there is a crisis.

Several provinces and many Canadian municipalities have strengthened heritage property legislation recently, so there are more tools available today. There are also heritage tax credit programs that have been initiated, which provide some assistance to property owners in recognition of the higher costs of maintaining such heritage properties.

Municipalities are also becoming more active in doing heritage property inventories, ranking heritage buildings according to importance and condition, and adding properties to lists that designate by category a community's heritage inventory.

A proactive stance is almost always more effective in preserving and protecting heritage properties. Education of building owners is important. More protection may be afforded by designating a property, or even a large area (one Ontario city has designated an entire neighbourhood of more than a thousand homes as a heritage conservation district).

In the downtown, buildings that come down can leave a "gap-tooth" streetscape that is unattractive and sets dangerous precedents. Sometimes, these properties then get turned into surface parking lots, which can also diminish efforts to refurbish a street. A vibrant downtown needs a vigorous, pulsing pedestrian presence and feel – not buses and cars spewing exhaust from a parking lot or street.

If a building can't be saved – and sometimes that is the reality – then a municipality should work with the local heritage community to do what can realistically be accomplished. Perhaps a façade can be saved, while the building structure behind is torn down and reconstructed. Sometimes, refurbishing the front can save the streetscape. Sometimes, replica facades using modern building techniques and materials can provide a reasonable alternative.

And, if a building can't be saved, then it is still important to defend the rest of the streetscape by insisting upon urban design considerations to protect neighbouring buildings from inappropriate new development. Developers are often willing to negotiate other community benefits, such as public art, providing public space, distinctive design features, or making a substantial cash contribution to the municipality's public art reserve fund – perhaps in exchange for a density bonus.

Local political leadership can play a strong role in representing the interests of a downtown, neighbourhood in stress, or heritage building or district.

Heritage buildings are a community treasure and resource. If your community is fortunate enough to have some, guard them and protect them.

Chapter 7

Development Partnerships and Opportunities

By Tim Jones

There is a tired old story about artists and gentrification that has been told and retold in major urban centres all over the world. It goes like this: Artists move into a downtrodden neighbourhood. They are attracted by cheap places to live and work, but they also see great value where others see dereliction. They begin to attract each other, and actively seek opportunities to share their enthusiasm for the place through their work. Before long, a market emerges for galleries, cafes, bars, and specialty retail. Once dull and dilapidated streets are transformed into energetic and vibrant districts, and real estate prices shoot through the roof.

Toronto Star urban affairs columnist Christopher Hume has likely written this story 40 or 50 times over the life of his career. Invariably, he's covering the displacement of a community of artists from a warehouse to make way for condominiums. Their low-rent status in a transformed commercial real estate context makes them prime targets for redevelopment. These stories are usually told with the same sad lament that casts artists as the hapless victims of the gentrification process they helped to spark.

Something Wrong with This Equation

In Canada, where the arts are at the heart of a creative economy that contributes $84.6 billion annually to the GNP, and employs 1.1 million people, there is something wrong with this equation. The core arts, cultural industries, and creative services that lifted Toronto's reputation from "Hogtown" to a highly ranked, dynamic urban centre remain under-served by public policy and investment, and struggle perpetually for survival. This is related to the more specific issue I will focus on:

how to affect systemic change in the relationship between the arts and the real estate market.

Conventional wisdom about the plight of artists in the path of gentrifying neighbourhoods is that very little can be done about it. In the urban development community, it is common to hear planners, developers, and councillors talk about the displacement of artists from the places that they enlivened as part of the natural evolution process. But, it is hardly appropriate to celebrate a phenomenon where the group that adds so much to property values consistently gets the raw end of the deal in the real estate market. Their nomadic condition results in repeated workplace disruption, and being relegated to the margins of urban life, where they are disconnected from other creative people and the marketplace. This cycle not only perpetuates the poverty of artists, but it diminishes their capacity to add value over time to local communities. If the development community took a longer view of the situation, it would realize the people being displaced were essential in retaining the vibrancy and authenticity of neighbourhoods and, therefore, in preserving real estate values.

Rise of Studio Providers

A new type of arts service organization known as "studio providers" began to emerge in the 70s and 80s to address the space challenges of urban artists. Artscape was created in 1986 in response to the space crisis faced by Toronto's arts community. At the time, the real estate market was in an extended boom, and the city began cracking down on illegal work and live/work spaces for artists. Artscape's original mandate was to provide safe, affordable, and secure space for the arts community. It followed the model pioneered by groups like Minneapolis's Artspace Projects and London's ACME and Space. It began leasing then subleasing work and live/work units to artists and small- and mid-sized arts organizations. Over 20 years, Artscape developed eight multi-tenant arts complexes that provide hundreds of spaces for the arts at below market rates.

Studio providers have become part of the infrastructure that is essential in sustaining a "Creative City." They anchor the arts in downtown communities and provide platforms for collaboration and resource sharing. But, while studio providers may offer an invaluable service, they face stiff competition for government and philanthropic support. In places where affordable studio providers exist, only a tiny fraction of the arts community can be accommodated in their limited facilities. Providing an affordable studio to an artist can help relieve their poverty, but it doesn't necessarily change their condition or position on the margins of urban life. Affordable space initiatives are a welcome band-aid to the real estate woes of the artistic community, but they don't fundamentally address the unfairness of the equation.

Borrowing a Page from the Social Enterprise Movement

Social enterprise is about advancing systemic solutions to major social problems. In recent years, it has become a global movement tackling issues of poverty, health, economic development, child welfare, etc. The traditional approach to solving what is wrong has followed a sequence very familiar to public and not-for-profit institutions: identify a need, raise the money to address it, build the capacity to respond, deliver the program to address the need. Social entrepreneurs, by contrast, are driven not just to serve the need; they are determined to solve the problem.

In his book *How to Change the World: Social Entrepreneurs and the Power of New Ideas,* David Bornstein argues "that it takes creative individuals with fixed determination and indomitable will to propel innovation that society needs to tackle its toughest problems."

His book shows that "an important social change frequently begins with a single entrepreneurial author: one obsessive individual who sees a problem and envisions a new solution, who takes the initiative to act on that vision, who gathers resources and builds organizations to protect and market that vision, who provides the energy and sustained focus to overcome the inevitable resistance, and who – decade after decade – keeps improving, strengthening, and broadening that vision until what was once a marginal idea has become a new norm."

Bornstein's observation on creative entrepreneurship provides a perfect description of the spirit and ambition that drives the Artscape team to effect systemic change: passionately interested in the role of the arts in regenerating neighbourhoods, building cities, and growing the new economy; appreciating that the arts generate enormous value – too little of which is reinvested in the health of the sector; and committed to rethinking and reframing this dysfunctional equation by applying the principles and lessons of social enterprise.

Defining a New Value Proposition

Changing the story about artists and urban development begins with recognizing that they are not hapless victims of the gentrification process, but are, in fact, powerful agents of change. If they are capable of generating cultural, social, and economic value, and driving neighbour-

63

hood revitalization, there should be a better deal that can be made. Artscape first demonstrated this in The Distillery district, where its involvement as the first major anchor tenant helped frame the value proposition and accelerate the momentum for this culture-led regeneration project. In exchange for the value Artscape contributed in advancing this initiative, it secured a below-market lease for 50,000 square feet for a mix of artists, designer/makers, and organizations. It's a deal that worked for the developers, the city, Artscape, and its tenants, because it was built to serve the common interest for all of the parties.

Artscape's experience with The Distillery and other recent projects has led to a major shift in the organization's approach. It has moved beyond the narrow focus and mindset of a studio provider to serve the space needs of artists. Today, Artscape may be considered a not-for-profit creative urban development group that harnesses the power of the arts to revitalize buildings, neighbourhoods, and cities. Artscape's work connects people, places, and ideas to generate cultural, economic, social, and environmental bottom lines. The quadruple bottom-line approach represents a new value proposition for all parties.

For Artscape, the best way to serve the needs and interests of Toronto's arts community is to align them with a broader set of agendas. In some cases, that may mean finding shared interest with condominium developers; in others, it may mean working with others interested in community economic development, urban planning, or some other public policy objective.

As Artscape has evolved as an organization, its constituency and relevancy have expanded. Today, the Artscape community is made up of a diverse group of members, partners, investors, stakeholders, and connectors who share an interest in building creative, vibrant, and resilient communities. Three categories of members who work and/or live at Artscape projects are the core of this community: artists, not-for-profit arts organizations, and associates. Artscape projects facilitate an exchange of value between Artscape members and a group of partners, investors, and stakeholders. Artscape brokers this exchange by developing creative space projects that also serve the interests of the broader community.

Unlocking Creative Potential of People and Places

Translating the new value proposition into projects that build the city and serve multiple interests requires creativity and knowledge. It is not something that can be effectively done by a group that positions itself exclusively as an advocate for the arts. To be an effective broker,

Artscape has evolved into a new breed of "intermediary" organization and has developed the competency to communicate in the language of developers, planners, community activists, economic developers, etc.

Artscape has also learned many lessons about how value can be constructed from arts and cultural assets. One of these is about the power of ideas to attract interest in an investment. Projects rooted in a compelling idea and supported by a spectacular design have a much stronger chance of happening than those driven by more modest aspirations.

Another important lesson from our work relates to people power. Individually, an artist or small arts organization may have very little capacity to generate cultural, economic, social, or environmental impact on a scale likely to attract investment. However, collectively, a group of creative people and organizations banded together can have an impact much bigger than the sum of their individual parts. The following two $20 million projects under development by Artscape illustrate this point.

1. Artscape Wychwood Barns

Artscape's adaptive re-use of a former Toronto Transit Commission streetcar repair facility marks the first intentional use of the quadruple bottom line value proposition. This city-owned site sat as a derelict industrial site in the heart of a residential neighbourhood for the better part of 30 years. Working with creative, environmental, and local community members, Artscape helped forge an aspirational vision for the project. On a practical level, the complex will provide 60,000 square feet of affordable space for a dynamic mix of arts, environmental, food security, recreation, and affordable housing uses. The project has been designed to provide a dynamic platform for cultural collaboration, strengthening the local economy, enriching the social fabric, and promoting a cleaner, greener environment. Individually, few if any of the hundreds of individuals and organizations involved in this project had the resources, knowledge, or power to make it happen. Working together with a strong and compelling vision, they have been able to attract the interest and investment to make it happen. Artscape Wychwood Barns opened in November 2008 after an 18 month-long renovation at a cost of $21.2 million.

2. Artscape Queen West Triangle

The area known as the Queen West Triangle has been one of the most intense development battlegrounds in recent history, pitting developers against artists, community activists, and the city. After years of squabbling and expensive legal wrangling, Artscape forged a win-win-win deal over lunch with community activists and one of the developers who was subsequently approved by the city. The project, now under construction, will allow Artscape to purchase 70 artist live/work units in a condominium. To make the deal work, Artscape pioneered a new self-financing model for affordable housing development that achieves affordability for renters without requiring government investment.

At its core, this project is about affordable space. But, the reasons it became a sound investment were different for each of the parties. For the developer, it was about securing a revenue neutral deal that satisfied city planning and employment objectives. For the city, it was about achieving objectives concerning mixed use and creative employment. Community activists were looking to ensure that artists remain part of the mix in the neighbourhood. All parties were looking for a better end to the story, in a way that builds the city. While this project is different in many ways from the Wychwood Barns, it also is designed to have cultural, economic, social, and environmental bottom lines.

Scaling Up Our Success

After many years of solid, incremental growth, Artscape is being encouraged to think bigger almost everywhere it turns. New developers, community activists, politicians, and city-builders beat a path to Artscape's door on a weekly basis. Like many other successful social enterprises, the major challenge ahead will be how to take its new mission to scale so that Artscape can deliver the kind of systemic change it envisions.

Artscape's leadership recognizes that getting there will require four things:

1. We will continue to invest in knowledge development and exchange, in an effort to support a virtuous cycle of growth between our knowledge, leadership, communications, and action.

2. We will work to heighten the level of engagement of our community of members, partners, investors, and stakeholders in our work.

3. We will launch a new Artscape Generates campaign to attract the resources that will help remove the barriers to new project development.

4. We will develop new methodologies to monitor and measure the quadruple bottom lines generated by Artscape's work.

With a freshly-minted new value proposition and more than a dozen projects in its development pipeline, Artscape is poised to lead the next wave of Toronto's cultural renaissance.

Chapter 8

Planning and Placemaking Tools

Shaping the neighbourhoods and communities of the future is one of the most important responsibilities of any municipal council.

Cultural Planning is at the heart of good, sustainable development. Bad development is often the result of poor Cultural Planning, and it can have consequences that ravage a community.

One enormous example is the Saint Roch neighbourhood of Quebec City. It was utterly devastated by bad urban planning decisions 40 years ago. The once-charming neighbourhood in the lower city was split apart by a new freeway that slashed through and destroyed heritage properties and communities, and forced huge concrete masses into the area. Then, as the neighbourhood deteriorated, desperate merchants on St. Joseph Street were convinced to ban traffic and dome the street with an ugly roof in a pathetic effort to create a downtown mall. It was a disaster.

The community, local political leaders, Quebec City's planning department, and the media all demanded change. The provincial government provided significant dollars, as did the municipal government. Institutions and the private sector came on side. Innovative design was utilized. Considerable courage was shown.

Today, the rejuvenation of Saint Roch is a shining example of good Cultural Planning. Welcoming the new core of arts and artisans, high-tech, education and culture, the neighbourhood is a delight. There is a huge park with a beautiful, tumbling water feature, ample open space for public events, and a vibrant street presence with cafes, patios and lots of "feet on the street." The $400 million cost has been roughly split between government and private sector investments.

There has been something of a small revolution going on in recent years in many North American communities. There has been a growing belief that we can do better – in civic design, in creating neighbourhoods that are socially friendly and more environmentally conscious, in redeveloping strong downtown cores, in designing houses that are greener and leaner, in opening bicycle trails and walking paths through the community, in increasing housing density, and in reducing the use of cars while increasing the availability of public transit.

Developers and builders are gaining a new appreciation for protecting natural heritage features in new developments. Rather than cutting trees and levelling mounds, smart builders are realizing that many people prefer (and will pay for) treed lots and homes that respect the environment, and they offer those amenities as part of new home developments.

Vancouver-based planning expert Larry Beasley has noted when he speaks to councils and administrators that, "Developers can be your friends." His point is absolutely valid – council members and staff who want to battle developers are missing the key point: make them partners in planned growth and positive urban development.

Smart communities today are working with developers to advance civic planning and placemaking goals. (Placemaking, for municipal purposes, is defined as an urban design process aimed at creating neighbourhoods that offer a strong sense of community, including a distinct character, healthy lifestyles, and a high quality of life.) Such goals may include:

► more compact urban development;

► bolder urban design, including greener initiatives for homes;

► an emphasis on pedestrian-friendly streets and corridors;

► variety and diversity in the housing mix, demographic diversity, and architectural design and creativity – a clear community vision for the subdivision or development;

► contributing to the creation of new, high-quality public spaces;

► doing interesting public art;

► innovative design, such as residential + retail + public space in the same complex;

► supporting public transit usage through the design and building process; and

► preserving natural environmental features.

This is truly a win-win-win situation. The municipality gets to meet its planning and economic objectives, the neighbourhoods receive responsible growth and development, and the risk-takers get a reasonable return on their investment.

The neighbourhoods of tomorrow are being created today, and it takes this partnership to ensure that we are producing livable, green, safe, and sustainable communities.

Community groups are an important part of this process. Their input, often at the earliest stages of a new community or area plan, is important. And, sophisticated community groups are realizing more frequently that "anti-everything" and "not in my (our) backyard" aren't responsible positions. It is a standing joke amongst local politicians that "everybody supports infill projects – until it happens on their street!" The best neighbourhood action groups are often the ones who want to be at the table to help shape the development, not reflexively oppose it.

The business sector will drive much of the growth and development in every community, and construction-related jobs are a substantial part of every local economy. Good developers want to be part of the process and work with their community. They are the ones risking the capital investment.

It is the municipality's job to set the overall guidelines through its official plan, to encourage innovation in building and design, and to approve orderly growth through zoning by-laws. A municipality can also challenge, inspire, support, lead, and assist in growth, development, and re-development – and in designing the buildings and neighbourhoods of tomorrow.

Working together, the community, developers, and builders offer a vastly stronger alliance. It sends a powerful message to council when both local residents and the developer agree and support the plan. Yet, too many municipal politicians automatically see a combative relationship between and amongst developers, builders, neighbourhood associations, environmental groups, and simply citizens concerned with and interested in building a strong, prosperous community.

There are other political positions besides "pro-development" or "anti-growth." Too often, media or local commentators attempt to pigeon-hole politicians into these opposite camps, making progress more difficult.

A "pro-business" politician can be very concerned about environmental issues; an "anti-growth" politician can still support jobs, new assessment growth and economic development ... so how do they find that sensible common space?

A Creative Community offers a prudent middle ground by recognizing the importance and necessity of working with developers and businesses, while encouraging innovative design, respecting the environment, and building safe, friendly neighbourhoods.

And, a municipality through its Cultural Planning report can offer strong leadership in several key planning areas.

Official Plan

The municipal process will likely start with including "Creative City" principles in the official plan. This will be an important recommendation in the Cultural Plan presented to and approved by the council. It is a huge step forward for a municipality seeking to embrace "Creative City" initiatives, and sends a powerful message. It enshrines the overall principles of good Cultural Planning in this critical document, and it clarifies that these principles are now part of the municipal planning process.

Zoning By-laws

A review of existing zoning may identify a number of by-laws that need to be updated or modified. For example, does the current by-law permit live/work/play/display apartments in sectors of the community, such as the downtown? By freshening the necessary zoning by-laws, the municipality sends a clear message of support and leadership for Cultural Planning.

Heritage Designations

Once a heritage property priority inventory has been taken, the municipality's next logical step is to encourage property owners to apply for heritage designation. Whether it is a lovely old home, the unique architecture of a stately downtown office building, or an entire neighbourhood of beautifully restored houses, preserving and protecting a community's built heritage is an important responsibility of council that also sends a critical message that this is a Creative Community with a commitment to its unique heritage buildings.

Urban Design Guidelines

Several leading communities have implemented urban design guidelines to "raise the bar" of architectural design and innovation. The effort is a response to the "cookie cutter" designs that have overwhelmed too many parts of too many communities. Normally, this process will involve peer-review panels of professionals (not politicians) reviewing plans. The general response has been to elevate design standards in both the private and public sectors – an approach welcomed by the general public and by the industry. The initiative can come out of the Cultural Plan Report and its recommendations.

Placemaking Demonstrations

Enlightened communities are today encouraging placemaking demonstrations for new and quite innovative neighbourhood developments. These demonstrations encourage a complete rethinking of traditional developments. For instance, they encourage more walking inside the neighbourhood, front porches, perhaps back alleys, transit-friendly communities, smaller homes, and a more eco-friendly design. Storm water management ponds become features with interesting parkettes and playgrounds; land use is more compact; and there may be gateways to the neighbourhood. The objective is safer, friendlier, and more environmentally-sensitive and sustainable neighbourhoods.

Many "Creative City" initiatives and ideas throughout this book are intended to provoke a new way of looking at communities and municipal governments, and how they do business. A planning department that is innovative, enterprising, and open to new ideas can become a vital partner in promoting Cultural Planning in any size community.

Communities are now recognizing that we need to re-think some of the old ways of doing business. Paving over green spaces in suburban areas is not usually the best solution. Promoting denser growth in the downtown and encouraging more sustainable forms of living and growing are all responsible actions by a council. It is to the planning department that much of the leadership will fall.

Developing new partnerships for economic development purposes is another key component of "Creative City" thinking. With the increasing financial pressures on municipalities, more and more public-private partnerships are being considered.

It is not unusual anymore for, say, a YM/YWCA to link with a new library and community centre to support a growing part of the community. The construction costs will be shared, development charges utilized as a funding vehicle for much of the public portion, a private sector manager may be responsible for the construction project, and the Y could end up running the entire facility.

Incentive Programs

To support a downtown revitalization project or process, the planning department may recommend some important initiatives. Municipal grants/loans vary significantly from community to community, but here are some concrete examples of incentive programs from Canadian municipalities.

1. Create an enterprise zone – The enterprise zone may be a broad section of the downtown (or other designated area), or may target a specific street or area. This designation can allow greater incentives that are funded by the public purse in recognition of the importance of that area – and of the eventual economic benefits to the community.

Recognizing that there are many different issues inside an enterprise zone, the solutions will be equally varied.

2. Brownfields – Various levels of government have programs available to assist in cleaning up these contaminated sites, often from former manufacturing operations that are long-closed. With stringent environmental laws today holding property owners potentially liable, these sites can sit vacant and rotting for decades. Reclaiming them is good for assessment growth, and rejuvenates a dead site.

3. Façade loans – Such loans assist property owners in certain designated areas with public money to renovate/repair store-front façades. The concept is to brighten and improve the streetscape. Loans would be repaid (often these are offered interest-free) over a five- or 10-year-period, or put on the tax rolls. Some municipalities may forgive up to 50 percent of the loan over time.

4. Awning, signage, and decorative lighting grants – This program provides financial assistance to property owners in designated areas to help bring buildings into conformity with the local property standards by-law. The grant might cover 50 percent of the cost (to a maximum of $X thousand) to help pay for upgraded awnings, signs, and lighting. It helps to improve the streetscape, and to upgrade the enterprise zone buildings.

5. Building Code loans – One of the most significant challenges to property owners trying to upgrade their (older) properties is meeting the new Building Code standards. This can be a major impediment to building owners. A municipal loan program can provide (perhaps) up to $50,000 (or half the cost) of these building improvements. The loan can be repaid over 10 years, without interest. Loans may be secured through a lien placed on title. Some municipalities may even forgive some or the entire loan if the building is located in certain enterprise zones and meets municipal conditions.

6. Accessibility loans – Assuring full accessibility – especially for older buildings that are in the downtown and that may have narrow doors, steps or stairways, and non-sidewalk-level street fronts – can be challenging. Many municipalities and provinces are now aggressively pursuing fuller accessibility for all residents, and are assisting building owners by providing loans on a 50-50 basis to encourage them to update their accessibility.

7. Heritage building assessment grants – A significant impediment for many building owners is simply trying to find out what physical condition their older building is in. Some municipalities are now assisting them by providing grants to help them conduct a full building (engineering) assessment of the structure with respect to the conservation/restoration of the building's heritage features.

8. Heritage building improvements grants – To encourage owners to protect, maintain, and restore their heritage properties, cash grants may be offered by municipalities. The grants would usually be restricted to buildings with a high heritage designation, and would be dependent upon the construction respecting and improving the heritage features. Typical grants might be for roof repairs, or removing aluminum siding that hides the original architectural features.

9. Development charge exemptions – To encourage building new residential structures in a moribund downtown or area, the municipality may provide a temporary holiday on development charges for new construction. The advantage to the municipality is bringing new assessment on-line, as well as a vibrant new residential tower to a designated area. The developer can save a substantial amount of money by not having to pay development charges. The municipality gets many decades of tax revenue.

10. Tax holiday grant – To provide specific incentives for targeted areas, a municipality may offer a tax holiday program for a few years. The program is likely to be quite specific – targeting new ground-floor retail space in designated buildings in an enterprise zone, for example. The incentive would attempt to attract a grocery store, perhaps, into an area that does not have food services. Often, these areas are economically disadvantaged.

Other grants, loans, and incentives may be provided from time to time. Provinces and municipalities often have limits on what kind of programs can be offered, but innovative thinking aimed at specific community objectives can be effective. The programs are often administered or promoted by the business improvement area board (BIA, Main Street, etc.).

Incorporating these planning ideas and incentive programs may at first be unusual in a "Creative City" process, but it soon becomes evident that you can't build or re-build a community without fundamental principles and programs in place.

Involving the planning department in the development of a Municipal Cultural Plan provides expertise that is important to the final recommendations.

It is important to note here that incentive programs and permissions will vary from province to province. There may also be requirements to tie the programs to the preparation of a community improvement plan for designated areas or districts. Provincial planning legislation and policies may give municipalities expanded authority to offer incentive programs, and to acquire and dispose of lands.

As Tim Jones detailed in Chapter 7, the tremendous successes of ArtScape's projects have proven that discovering innovative "wins" for everyone is a powerful planning tool. Using the rules and zoning issues to advantage is clever. Taking advantage of incentive programs helps advocates and owners. Seeking partners for projects and involving community advocates helps to ensure broader acceptance, and the chance of success.

The conclusion is plain. Working with the Planning department to find innovative solutions and advocate for bold concepts will afford a greater chance of success.

Chapter 9

Public Art

Public art can inspire, excite, stimulate, provoke, titillate, awaken, arouse, animate, disgust, thrill, whet, perturb, incite, insight, demand, deny, and electrify.

There are times when public art can amuse, bemuse, and confuse.

In remarkable cases, public art becomes the iconic face of a community – the famous Eiffel Tower in Paris, for example, or the magnificent Christ the Redeemer statue that overlooks the harbour in Rio de Janeiro, Brazil.

Public art, at its grandest, certainly has the potential to enliven, enhance, and enchant. Public spaces can be changed, and the public spirit can be elevated. Leading civilizations, from the Chinese dynasties to the Italian Renaissance period, have left us with inspiring pieces of art.

Often, they are representative of the culture and history of a community, such as Heroes' Square in Budapest, Hungary that celebrates the magnificent thousand-year history of the Magyars, or the Terra Cotta Warriors of Xi'an, China that honour that country's first emperor in 210 BC.

Surely, progressive communities have no less a responsibility today.

Many communities take this obligation very seriously. They understand that, while a community needs roads and sewers, it also needs investment and leadership in its spirit and culture.

There is an artistic and cultural infrastructure to be built, as well as the physical and technological infrastructures of a community.

It isn't an "either-or" argument. Public art and celebrating our cultural achievements are simply part of modern, intelligent society. Art, music, sculptures, urban design, natural and built heritage, writings – in other words, culture in the fullest sense – are the things that help to civilize our communities. They make life more enjoyable. They celebrate the human spirit, and the remarkable accomplishments of artists and artisans.

In Ukraine, there are statues of poets. Greece honours its philosophers. The wonders of the Mayan culture are still being discovered in Guatemala and Mexico. From the delicacy of calligraphy scrolls in Japan to the stupendous Machu Pichu in Peru, the world is filled with examples of great public art. And, we are the better for it.

Yet, for municipalities embarking upon public art policies and projects today, these can be surprisingly shark-infested waters.

Figure Out Where You're at with Public Art

This is the starting point, and it may surprise you how uncertain the answer(s) may be:

Do you have a public art policy? Is it recent, or some dusty version that hasn't been followed in decades?

Does the municipality have an inventory of public art? Astonishingly, many municipalities don't have an up-to-date inventory or record.

Who's responsible for the existing public art? Is there somebody at city hall who administers the policy? Who cleans the art, protects it, and preserves it?

Is there a budget for public art? Who administers it? Who spends it? What if you need or want to de-commission public art? (Public art is not necessarily permanent.)

Is there a reserve fund for public art? What would you do if some nice person left the municipality $100,000 for public art in his or her will?

Cultural Plan and Recommendations

Include a chapter on public art in your Cultural Plan Report and Recommendations. This gives the municipality a chance to review, update, or introduce a policy on public art.

Get the community roused in favour of public art. There will always be nay-sayers … you need some positive support to move the agenda forward.

One Percent Solution

Consider having the municipal council adopt a policy of contributing one percent annually to a public art fund through the annual operating budget. The one percent is based upon (for example) major applicable above-ground capital works projects. In other words, a $10 million capital budget for the municipality would result in a $100,000 contribution to public art.

It may be easier to adopt an agreeable figure based on average municipal capital spending, then develop an annual budget commitment based upon that amount (+ inflation) that becomes part of the core operating budget of the municipality. The final step is to then create a reserve fund, so that funding not used in one year for public art can be banked for use during another year (for example, if a municipality wanted to save-up to finance a really major piece of public art). That reserve fund could also accept donations or bequests from the public, or contributions from developers (see below).

Allow for Private Sector Participation

There is a strong argument for allowing the private sector to receive density bonuses in exchange for contributions to the public art reserve fund, or for committing to provide public art in the new or renovated building. These projects could include special design features, adding public space, water features, innovative lighting, or cash contributions to the municipality's public art reserve fund.

De-Politicize the Process

Make it an early commitment to get artistic decisions on public art out of city hall!

The simplest way to do that may be to make an arrangement with the local arts council to take over the responsibility to receive the applications, jury the finalists, etc. You don't want councillors debating public art projects – if they do, the three-ring circus of media sensationalism, coupled with public meetings, fuelled by political controversy, will surely ensue!

You want to make these investments a standard part of the project. For example, London's public art policy states, "For City of London capital projects over the value of $1 million, investment in public art should be considered as part of that project." In other words, public art investments should become the norm for municipalities, not the exception.

Be Prepared for Negative Feedback

Not everyone will love every public art project. Some will argue based upon the "sewers not art" fallacy. Some will hate the piece. Some will scream you're wasting their hard-earned dollars. Be comforted ... not everyone liked the Eiffel Tower in Paris when it was built.

Many people share an inherent belief that arts and culture are what civilize our world. Is it reaching too far to wonder if the 2008 visit by the

New York Philharmonic to Pyongyang will help to ease diplomatic pressures between the United States and North Korea?

Public art reflects a community and its people. Art and artisans provide unique mirrors and insights into our world today.

Canadian municipalities have done some excellent work in recent years on developing and implementing public art policies. While themes are similar, approaches can vary. To review five interesting policies from municipalities of differing sizes, check out the following municipal websites, and follow the links to get their policies on public art:

1. Calgary, AB <www.calgary.ca>

2. Port Moody, BC <www.cityofportmoody.com>

3. Winnipeg, MB <www.winnipegarts.ca>

4. London, ON <www.london.ca>

5. Vancouver, BC <www.vancouver.ca

The public art photo contest that Municipal World conducted in conjunction with this book publication resulted in an amazing 71 entries from municipalities across Canada. We were able to select only 10 to share with readers as part of this publication. These represent only a fraction of the innovative public art that is out there. We were so impressed with the response that we are now exploring ways we might do this again, to support and develop a greater appreciation of civic and public art in communities across Canada.

Chapter 10

Social, Environmental, and Community Challenges

A growing concern and responsibility for Canadian municipalities is the increasing number of social, environmental, and community challenges that they face today.

Done well, Cultural Planning can provide answers and assistance to some of these societal ills. A fundamental belief of those of us in this business is that a Creative Community is also a Healthy Community.

Members of the Creative Class are quite environmentally conscious and sensitive, as the research into the needs and wants of Gen X and Y has proven. So, the ability to live in a green district will be one of their considerations when deciding what kind of community will attract their talents. Municipal leaders must therefore be aware and proactive about the kind of community they are creating, because sense of place is an important factor in attracting and retaining these desirable and mobile residents.

A community that offers cultural opportunities, a lively arts presence, a strong downtown, fun clubs, bars and restaurants, social opportunities, a robust economy, and intellectual stimulation is more likely to attract these leaders. But, the community must also offer a healthy ambience and a commitment to a cleaner environment.

Emerging social issues, such as childhood obesity, the stunning increase in Type 2 diabetes in Canada, the huge jumps in oil and energy prices, and the demands for a greener community in a greener world, may initially seem like strange Cultural Planning partners. But, in fact, they are representative of the "Creative City" thinking for progressive communities.

For example, if we can design neighbourhoods that promote walking, biking, and a strong neighbourhood spirit, then reasonable expectations would include:

► less use of cars, especially single occupancy vehicles (SOVs) – with fewer SOVs meaning savings on road costs to build, clean, and repair;

► promoting use of public transit;

► a family environment in neighbourhoods, resulting in stronger family units and safer neighbourhoods (for example, front porches to help keep an eye on strangers);

► walking and biking trails to encourage fitness and healthy living;

► designing community gardens and parks in these neighbourhoods to encourage families to respect local food sources, the natural and built environment, and again promote a healthier lifestyle;

► building Energy-Star homes to save on heating and cooling costs, which, in turn, use less energy and some non-renewable resources;

► garden plots for apartment dwellers;

► green roofs for downtown buildings;

► and so on.

It is more of this new way of thinking about municipal governance that this book is urging. It is forcing municipal councils to do business in new and different ways. It is engaging the local developers and home builders as partners, instead of as "the enemy."

Whether it is dense urban high-rise neighbourhoods or new subdivisions, Canadian cities and towns are starting to push for better quality urban design, environmental sensitivity, community and neighbourhood consultation, creative thinking, and healthier communities. These are desirable and attainable outcomes for good civic Cultural Planning.

Voters today are demanding more leadership from their local elected officials in this area. What was once left to other orders of government are today very much "on the street" realities for local officials. Their constituents are very clear – social, environmental, and health issues are important to them, and to their families.

"Creative City" thinking provides many answers for municipalities. Voters like the extensive community outreach that goes into developing the plan. It quickly becomes a community-based strategy. The local council members are positioned as real leaders.

This shift in municipal thinking also resonates with the civic administration. It makes them review things such as the parks and recreation master plan (or whatever strategic document there may be) through eyes that are wide open.

If we are going to have newer design and development in neighbourhoods, what will that mean for our traditional civic facilities?

► Should municipalities be building larger regional facilities, or a greater number of smaller neighbourhood facilities?

► Are libraries and community centres, for example, better combined together, or should we build stand-alone facilities spread across the community?

► As the population ages, what shifts in recreation focus will result? Fewer hockey rinks and tennis courts, more golf courses, soccer fields, and community garden plots? More walking/biking trails? Paved bike lanes on streets or sidewalks?

► Alternatively, some Canadian cities are developing walking paths inside buildings, as Calgary has done with its interesting elevated walkway system that now includes 57 bridges above the street and 16 kilometres of public walkways.

► What about outdoor strength fitness facilities on community trails?

► How does an urban area "green" its community and recreation facilities in a sea of concrete?

► How are sustainable communities going to be developed and maintained?

► How do we assist small neighbourhood projects? (Things like landscaping a public housing project, for example.)

► How do municipalities reach out to immigrants more and welcome them into the community?

► How do civic facilities adapt to the needs of their changing populations? (For example, providing female-only swimming times at public pools.)

► How does a community preserve and protect its watershed to ensure a healthy source of water, a pleasant recreational amenity, and a community focus and feature?

► How do municipalities continue to encourage and expand waste reduction and recycling?

These are just a few of the many emerging issues for municipalities.

Municipal governments have a steadily increasing number of challenges, and that's why progressive local councils are changing the way they think, work, communicate, and plan.

Cultural Planning is moving away from the distant shores into the daily mainstream of city halls.

LEED Standards

A strong leadership statement for a local council to make comes in the design and construction of new public facilities. The new standard is LEED: Leadership in Energy and Environmental Design.

This is a point-based system of design and building to encourage energy savings, reusable resources, lower greenhouse gas emissions, use of solar energy, and so on. The highest level is platinum.

Attaining a LEED standard is a worthwhile and achievable goal for municipalities as they construct new community facilities.

Calgary did a brilliant job with the construction of its Cardel Integrated Community Centre. The complex offers swimming/wading/hot tubs, a gymnasium, two ice pads, a library, and a day care facility. It achieved gold LEED status through a variety of effective design strategies – it has an ice battery for air conditioning during the day; it draws heat from the ice and uses that to heat the pool; the storm water management pond is used for irrigation; plus other innovative design features.

Kingston, Ontario achieved a LEED silver designation with its new police headquarters. The $27 million project is now open, and features a campus concept plan to also encompass other Kingston emergency services.

Trees and Woodlots

Communities are now introducing new by-laws dealing with protection of natural woodlots, and many communities now budget each year to acquire woodlots, floodplain lands, and other environmentally sensitive areas to ensure they will remain in the public domain.

Many new area development plans require the dedication of a certain percentage of those lands for public use, often through parks or natural areas. Municipalities are becoming increasingly protective of these natural heritage features, and the public often demands greater protection for trees and woodlots.

There is frequently some tension between the various parties as this plays out, and municipalities are taking positive actions to ensure environmental standards are met and maintained. There may be a strong push-back by community activist groups to protect certain trees or natural areas on new and in-fill projects, and councils are increasingly persuaded to accommodate those neighbourhood issues.

There is also a movement in many municipalities to plant new trees as a defined civic priority. Insect infestations are attacking some species (eg. Emerald Ash Borer in eastern Canada, or the Mountain Pine Beetle in British Columbia). Re-forestation is becoming a growing concern and expense for municipalities. Land stewardship is now high on the agenda for Canadian municipalities.

Conservation Programs

Municipalities are in a significant leadership role for energy savings — both as an example by their own usage, and by urging the broader community to save water, turn off the lights, conserve energy, and reduce greenhouse gases.

As the owners of the municipal water and sewage utilities, Canadian municipalities have a special interest in water conservation, while ensuring a reliable and ample supply of clean, safe water for residents. This is a significant core responsibility.

"Green programs" are now offered by most municipalities and/or utilities. These range from offering a small cash bonus and free pick-up of old, energy-inefficient "beer fridges," to encouraging builders to provide higher levels of insulation, windows, and other home energy savings programs.

Community Health Leadership

A number of municipalities have followed the lead of Hudson, Quebec in banning the cosmetic use of pesticides in their municipalities. In fact, some provincial governments are arriving late to the party — after municipalities have done the hard work — and are introducing provincial legislation to ban the use and even sale of many pesticides.

This same battle is being — and has been — played out for smoking in public facilities. Unless there is provincial government leadership, it will fall to municipalities to show the leadership in these kinds of public health concerns.

The problem for the various business sectors impacted, of course, is that municipalities develop their own by-laws, which will vary from town to city to rural area. If or when a provincial government then imposes its own legislation, it usually supersedes local by-laws. This means a whole new set of rules and regulations for business, industry, and homeowners. They are naturally frustrated and often have spent substantial money to improve facilities or change their operating procedures.

City Hall Leadership

Residents naturally expect their municipal leaders to show leadership in environmental matters. Its part of a healthy community, and that means a community that is appealing to the Creative Class.

Municipalities across Canada are showing great leadership in sustainable projects and policies, such as:

► developing a "green fleet" of municipal vehicles (traffic enforcement, etc);

► planting "green roofs" on municipal buildings;

► using "grey water" for certain functions;

► refitting community facilities with more energy efficient lights and HVAC systems;

► setting up marked walking/biking trails downtown to encourage physical fitness for office workers during their noon-hours;

► providing special secure bike racks for office workers, or regulating that parking garages must also provide a number of bicycle parking spaces;

► pressing manufacturers to reduce packaging materials (especially plastic bubble packaging) and shipping non-recyclables;

► reducing the usage of plastic bags;

► switching to more energy efficient street lights, as Dawson Creek, British Columbia did following a comprehensive energy audit;

► installing low flow toilets and urinals in public buildings;

► making innovative use of water holding tanks and ponds to supply some heating/cooling;

► undertaking energy audits for public facilities; and

► encouraging water conservation through lawn watering restrictions, collecting rain water and other methods, as Victoria, British Columbia has been doing for the last dozen years.

Other specific municipal examples include the following:

► The Charlesbourg Library in Quebec City developed a geothermal energy system for its heating/cooling, consisting of 21 underground boreholes each 150 metres deep.

- ▶ Edmonton, Alberta partnered with Petro Canada to start a marvelous plan to reuse waste water effluent by piping it five kilometres to a refinery where it is used to produce low sulfur diesel fuel.

- ▶ The Terra Nova Rural Park in Richmond, British Columbia is a terrific example of the community coming together to save, protect, and responsibly develop a large environmental area into four parks in one; the project has become an award-winner for the city.

- ▶ Calgary, Alberta has become the first North American community to power its transit system with 100 percent emissions-free wind-generated electricity.

- ▶ Waterloo, Ontario is raising a more aware generation by partnering with the local school boards to offer a Grade 3 curriculum supplement that educates children about transportation issues and greenhouse gases and emissions.

- ▶ Hamilton, Ontario established a "green cart" program for the recycling and collection of organic waste products.

- ▶ Craik, Saskatchewan is developing an eco-village concept for a new housing complex, featuring a rainwater capture system, composting toilets, and environmentally friendly interior finishing techniques.

- ▶ Halifax, Nova Scotia has implemented Climate SMART, a fully integrated planning approach that addresses the impact of climate change.

- ▶ Montreal, Quebec conducted an extensive community consultation campaign to help it develop a comprehensive five-year sustainability program, including such highlights as improving the city's cycling infrastructure.

- ▶ An early-stage commitment to introducing transit service for new developments, rather than waiting, has helped Brampton, Ontario to increase transit ridership by 40 percent in just four years.

There are many other examples from leading Canadians communities. Innovative ideas are being implemented and communities are responding to this leadership. The Creative Class is sensitive to, and serious about, environmental issues. Schools are educating a new generation of young citizens who will be even more demanding of governments for ecological improvements.

All orders of government have responsibilities to continually improve our environment, and to provide safe, clean, healthy, and environmentally-responsible communities in which citizens can live.

A Creative Community is also a Healthy Community.

Chapter 11

Changing the Thinking

Once you have your Cultural Plan put together and adopted by council, the hard work begins: changing the thinking – in city hall, in the community, in senior governments.

1. Changing the thinking with the municipal administration – Bureaucrats in any order of government are by nature and by circumstance (and perhaps by the infamous "system") protective, disciplined, and careful. Many are cautious. Very cautious.

But they are also capable of highly creative thinking, of constructive and thoughtful ideas and processes, and of rallying support for civic initiatives. You need their help for your plan and its implementation succeed.

The key is support from the top. You really need the support of the CAO or city manager (whichever is the top municipal civil servant) for the Cultural Plan.

Once council adopts the recommendations and establishes the policies, staff will likely want to come back to the council with an implementation strategy and timetable, perhaps budget estimates, and to assign tasks to various departments. Your CAO doesn't have to be hands-on in the implementation, but it is important for the senior management team – and indeed the entire organization – to understand clearly that Cultural Planning is now a policy of the council and has the full support of the CAO.

Administrators operate within policy guidelines. That's why it is crucial to have council adopt the Cultural Plan formally. That gives the civic administration the authority to proceed within those approved parameters.

You now have the council approval of your plan. You also have the administration's plan for implementation. Everything is great!

Well ... a few potential pitfalls remain.

2. Earning public acceptance and changing the thinking in the community – You need a well-developed communication strategy as part of the process.

It is crucial to have positive media support for the plan. The media must understand this complex issue. That means you must have a simple, clear, and consistent message for the media, and you must sell it proactively.

It may be useful to meet with the editorial boards of the local newspapers, even before the report is presented at council. Newspapers will usually agree to hold the information under embargo until the public presentation; but, meeting in advance with their senior editors and reporters gives you the chance to have a longer, more thoughtful discussion about the report and its importance – instead of in the pressurized crucible of a media scrum.

These are not simple or easy issues to explain, so make sure you have a couple of clear talking points. The average radio or television sound bite is about eight seconds. Reporters may also be young and inexperienced, so it will be important to help them to understand. Initial media spin is of tremendous importance in gaining community acceptance.

The follow-up is then an on-going communication effort – speeches at service clubs and community groups, debates at the local college and/or university, annual general meetings of cultural groups, and so on. Your objective is to help the community understand and accept the foundation of the report, and then the report's conclusions and recommendations.

Happily, there are lots of very smart people in the community who will not only understand the report and its importance to your community's future, but will want to be active supporters of (parts of) the report. Many community groups actually "adopt" one or two of the recommendations, and take possession of moving it forward. For example, the library system is a natural ally, and the library board may choose to establish its own Creative Community committee and/or policies.

What you are seeking is a complete, comprehensive action plan for communications that embraces all of the key target audiences with a consistent message.

*3. **Working with the arts/cultural/heritage sectors** – Changing the thinking for this group can be challenging. Your report may have recommended some changes in how these sectors are structured. It may have created new collaborations and partnerships. It may have brought together (perhaps for the first time) general managers and executive directors that thought they were competitors. It might have served notice to organizations fighting decades-old battles that they are stronger together.

Whatever the situation, this is the opportune moment to make sure these important sectors are structured properly. Take advantage of it – it is a rare opportunity to force or support change on an industry that too often resists restructuring.

This group can be a key source of support for the report. But, they must be together and present a united public front. Even if they have variances with an occasional phrase or recommendation in the final report, make sure they are supportive and responsive. Any small crack will give negative council members an opportunity to exploit a "divided community." The overall positive benefits of the report far, far outweigh any dispute over a particular issue. Make sure this group knows and understands this.

4. Changing that relationship with other key target audiences – The business community's role in all of this is a curious one. Some business leaders will instinctively get it and be supportive; others will be apathetic. Generally, they are going to see the advantages, the opportunities, and the possibilities, but may need help in understanding investment spending and why this is important to the community.

The academic community is another valuable source of support. There will tend to be much interest, because so much of what the Cultural Plan Report details will be based upon the academic/research/business/theatrical disciplines on campus. The emerging leaders and the Creative Class are students today – but they are the key players tomorrow.

The labour community will likely be mildly supportive. The downtown businesses and residents are likely to be strong supporters, because of the natural links with a robust downtown, and the activities the Creative Class enjoys.

Emerging leaders are a tremendously important target audience. Many of them have a strongly developed sense of responsibility, and want to give back to their community. Nurture this relationship.

5. Changing the thinking at budget time – Councils will often approve a policy or report, but refer the actual budget items to the annual budget process. While many "Creative City" initiatives don't require a lot of money – their ideas and energy push them forward naturally – there are some costs and some investments that must be made in implementing your Cultural Plan. It is important to have staff support and strong council leadership to help steer the budget requests through the shoals of the budget debate.

Expect attacks from the ill-informed councillors who will argue loudly, "... how can we spend one nickel on public art/"Creative City"/Cultural Planning, etc when: (i) roads and sewers are crumbling; (ii) people are starving on our streets; (iii) taxes are too high and seniors are losing their homes; (iv) the world as we know it is ending ... "

The response is simple. As we know now, Cultural Planning is very much about the economic future and prosperity of your community. It is economic growth that increases the assessment base, provides new taxes to municipal coffers, and generates the people and businesses that will attract the entrepreneurs, the Creative Class, and their economic strength and power.

This is also why smart communities are aligning their cultural office in the CAO or city manager's department. Structured this way, cultural departments aren't trying to compete with the other primary business units in the organization.

6. Changing the political thinking – You must have a champion for this at council. If the administration doesn't believe council thinks this is important, then they have lots of other work to do.

A champion on the council can ask the questions, help shape the political agenda, get budget dollars allocated, and be a strong public spokesperson for this change of thinking.

Political leadership still drives the agenda forward. There are many competing and worthwhile projects, activities, ideas, and directions at a municipal council. Making sure the Creative Community agenda remains active, moving forward, is vital to success.

Bringing Council Together

Cultural Planning is one of the few major issues that can easily bridge the left and right elements of a council.

The left wing supporters will quickly understand the benefits of higher density for residential development and of re-thinking the traditional sprawling suburban neighbourhoods. They will be supportive of strong downtowns, public art, and a vibrant arts and cultural sector. The right wing members will see the possibilities for higher assessment growth, more jobs for young people, a stronger local economy, and a progressive infrastructure program. And, while there may not be unanimity on council, there will certainly be a strong consensus. That's good enough to move this agenda forward.

Challenges Ahead

Inside city hall, lots of challenges lie ahead. However, changing the thinking is a positive step, and smart managers will realize that.

Starting any kind of new department or division will inevitably bring turf wars. That's why having the support and firm commitment of the CAO is important. The new culture office (or whatever it is called) will likely tap dollars and programs from existing departments where they have been scattered inefficiently and without focus. There will be some elbowing in the administrative corners; a wise councillor ignores this and remains focused on the council policy.

Each civic department has a role to play in implementing the Cultural Plan recommendations.

Engineering departments can let their creative juices flow – something that isn't always allowed to happen. Too often, their minds are constrained by linear thinking and budget pressures. "Creative City" thinking offers new vistas – in Calgary, for example, one highway overpass has metal sculptures of animals.

Engineering can also rise to the occasion with new designs for everything from sewage plants to pedestrian bridges. Innovative design, landscaping, and public amenities are all possibilities. And, why not involve the local university engineering students in a design competition for a public facility?

Engineering will also be involved in public programs, from street cleaning downtown to recycling and blue/green box programs. There's lots of creativity in your engineering department – just give them the opportunity.

Parks and recreation departments are intimately involved in implementing Cultural Planning recommendations. Parks and public spaces are critical elements in redefining any community. Programs – physical, artistic, cultural, and others – for children, seniors, disabled, and other groups are vital. New community facilities – such as a community centre, arena, library, or combination of public needs – provide a very special opportunity for attractive landscaping, public art, respecting the natural heritage, and leadership in environmental stewardship. Walking/biking trails are important to people.

Public housing projects have too often become a ghetto. Establishing pride in their neighbourhood, funding small initiatives, re-claiming control of playgrounds and community spaces, and providing a secure environment are important steps.

Planning departments have enormous influence on and responsibility for implementing the Creative Community policies. For example, zoning changes to accommodate live/work/play/display spaces; introducing heritage protection policies for buildings, often in the downtown; introducing Cultural Planning concepts into the official plan; leading the push for innovative urban design guidelines, and for creating more livable neighbourhoods – these are only some of the implementation opportunities from the planning department.

Public health has a role to play. Environmental concerns are often investigated by the public health department, and that department often presents health concerns and proposed policies to the community and to council. People are increasingly demanding civic leadership in developing healthier, safer communities. From non-smoking in public places to offering healthier street food, a Creative Community is a healthy community. And, an emerging issue – is your community age-friendly? In other words, as our society ages, are we designing communities and public facilities to accommodate the new and often very different demands of an aging population?

Tough questions emerge from a comprehensive Cultural Planning process. Don't shy away. Other important civic bodies also have key roles to play – particularly the **Economic Development** portfolios. What is the Canadian perception of your community? What are your tourist and convention people selling? Is your economic development department in sync with the changes you're making in your community? What competitive advantages can you now offer? Is your community an attractive destination for conventions and tourists? Do developers want to do business with your administration? Are foreign investors welcome in your community? What immigration levels are you attracting?

Whatever composition your municipal administration is, every department, agency, board, and commission is going to be involved in making and becoming a Creative Community. Their commitment and dedication to changing your community is paramount; without it, the plan's implementation will be diminished, and your community won't receive the full benefits. Fortunately, Canadian municipalities have many outstanding leaders in municipal government, and a solid core of innovative, creative, and dedicated administrative personnel.

One More Problem ...

Canadian municipalities are hot beds of culture, innovation, and wealth creation. Here's the problem: the federal and (most) provincial governments need to catch up and support these municipal initiatives.

There are some very clever civil servants in Ottawa that do understand this issue, but they need to be allowed to become champions for Cultural Planning. It is a matter of great frustration and disappointment for leading municipalities in Canada to have so few elected voices on Parliament Hill who understand, support, and champion the "Creative City" movement – or, indeed, municipal issues of any kind.

The federal government has offered the excellent Cultural Capitals of Canada program for the past several years. The program has various categories (by size) and allows Canadian municipalities to compete for cash and the title of a Cultural Capital. However, in 2008, the federal government announced devastating and sweeping cuts to various cultural programs of $60 million that galvanized the arts community across the country.

Provincial governments across Canada deal with municipalities in vastly different ways. There are signs of maturing, improving relationships in some provinces. More responsible and fairer funding is emerging, as there is a growing acknowledgement that the property tax base was simply never intended to pay for things like social programs and income redistribution schemes. But, the rebalancing is far from over, and municipalities need to remain proactive, vigilant, and aggressive.

Here's the basic problem – municipalities in Canada get only eight cents out of every tax dollar.

That is not sustainable, with the ever-growing demands for service and infrastructure spending. US cities have considerably more latitude in tax authority, and the federal government there invests billions of dollars in local communities.

The Canadian public *does* seem to get it. They understand that infrastructure in their communities is deteriorating. They also understand that the local tax base can't fund the billions of dollars needed to improve that infrastructure. There is widespread community support for infrastructure investments across Canada.

There is also support from the business community. The President and CEO of TD Bank Financial Group, Ed Clark, said in a 2008 speech, "It is the role of business to create the jobs and industries of the future. It is the role of government to invest in cities to make them attractive places in which to live and work. Cities are absolutely vital to strong economies."

Cultural Planning offers the possibility and the process for the community to come together and develop an exciting vision for the future. The "Creative City" thinking that develops the kinds of plans and vision that have been outlined in this book offers clear, unvarnished looks at your community and what it can become. And, perhaps *that* is going to become our new national vision – a network of municipalities that are bold, innovative, creative, and visionary in how they build the communities of tomorrow in which people will live and prosper.

A Creative Community will only be fashioned by strong local commitments to vision and to action. That means changing the thinking – at city hall and on the streets.

The Creative City Network of Canada is a national program of municipal cultural administrators and interested partners who exchange information and ideas, conduct seminars, and promote "Creative City" planning and implementation. It has had a very positive impact on Cultural Planning across Canada.

Another terrific provincial example in support of this movement is the Ontario Municipal Cultural Planning Partnership (MCPP), a unique concept that can be adapted for other provinces. The conglomeration brings together seven provincial ministries, the Association of Municipalities of Ontario, leading towns and cities, and the cultural/heritage/arts sectors together with private business. The priorities for the MCPP are to help towns and cities:

- ▶ support a stronger economic base and increase local assessment;

- ▶ help build robust, livable communities that are diverse and culturally strong; and

- ▶ integrate Cultural Planning as the fourth pillar of municipal decision making.

MCPP acts as a resource for Ontario municipalities and ministries, and supports them through information, education, research, and advocacy. Such an organization can also provide important generic background work for this emerging industry, such as setting professional standards for Cultural Planning, and gaining increased acceptance – and even some form of accreditation – in the planning profession for the standards and practices of consultants and municipal planning professionals.

We have the people at the municipal level to do this in Canada. We have the knowledge. We have the tools. Do we have the courage and dedication? And, do we have the commitment to pull together and compel our partners in the provincial and federal orders of government to work with us to make it happen? More on this in the next chapter.

Chapter 12

Strategic Planning, Priorities, and Success Indicators

Municipal Cultural Planning is still in its formative years. It is evolving and maturing, and will be for years to come. It is an art and a science and a philosophy, and it is gradually seeping into the mindsets of municipal politicians across North America, as it has done already in parts of Europe, Australia, and other countries.

The ultimate goal, of course, as has happened with the environmental movement, is that Cultural Planning simply becomes a routine, expected, and integral part of all discussions, debate, and decision making for local government. Cultural Planning has become the fourth pillar of sustainability for municipalities.

We don't know yet if the politicians will lead the public in this, or if the public will demand it of politicians. What seems clear, however, is that in a world and in a time of increased focus on community sustainability, the time is now for pushing forward with Municipal Cultural Planning in communities of all sizes.

Cultural Planning cuts across many traditional civic government walls and boundaries, and that makes it both exhilarating and challenging for many people. From changing a community's official plan to attracting the next generation of entrepreneurs from the Creative Class, Cultural Planning adds both breadth and depth to local policy making.

What seems indisputable, however, is that the "Creative City" movement is gathering momentum and support. The principles just make too much sense. The community-focused process this book recommends provides a special opportunity to re-shape a municipality's direction, focus, and strategic plan to take advantage of 21st century economic and cultural opportunities.

In an era of often diminished local tax resources, it is crucial for local councils to spend wisely, invest bravely, and lead decisively. Voters are demanding more and more from their local elected officials. They are entitled to that.

"Creative City" thinking offers a dynamic intersection of community and government.

Strategic Planning

Whether it is called "Creative City" thinking, "Municipal Cultural Planning," "Community Vitality," or some other name, it is important to get the principles endorsed in your municipality's official strategic plan. The community's vision statement should firmly recognize and support these concepts.

A strategic plan offers a broad direction to staff, the community, and the public. By including Cultural Planning in the overall strategic plan, it solidifies the authenticity and importance of this fourth pillar of sustainability. Acceptance and knowledge of Cultural Planning then begins to become routine, expected, and welcomed. Cultural Planning must become part of the regular decision making at city hall. All decisions should now be looked at through the cultural lens.

By nature, strategic plans are broad, general, and sweeping. The details come later in the action plan and the recommendations that council adopts. But, having the "Creative City" concepts included as part of a municipality's strategic initiatives is a huge step toward becoming a Creative Community.

Civic Priorities

A council's priorities are established through a combination of the strategic plan + council direction + the budget process. Community input is vital through all of these. That is also why having a Creative Community Committee or some other similar, formal civic group is important.

Appointed by council, and with both council and citizen representatives, this committee can serve as a watchdog for the implementation the Cultural Plan, and also as an information source for council members, and as an advocacy body for cultural and community issues. It can make sure civic priorities include recommendations from the adopted Cultural Plan, and push to get budget approval for specific items and initiatives.

A few council members and a much larger number of community representatives would be a good structure for the committee. Keeping the community engaged also ensures continued support for the Cultural Plan, and provides an opportunity for new input, fresh ideas, and interesting partnerships.

Indicators and Benchmarking

It is quite reasonable for council members and the community to want some indicators of progress/success with their Cultural Plan. Because this is an emerging concept, there is also an emerging set of indicators being developed. But, here are a few *quantifiable* indicators and statistics, some of which you may want to choose as your community's key indicators:

➤ assessment growth;

➤ housing starts (perhaps in selected areas, such as the downtown);

➤ immigration statistics;

➤ job creation/employment;

➤ tourism and convention visits and dollars spent;

➤ literacy rates;

➤ number and strength of arts and cultural organizations;

➤ community health indicators;

➤ economic development prospects;

➤ foreign investment;

➤ website visits;

➤ community festivals/events/attractions;

➤ attendance patterns at historic sites, museums, galleries, etc.;

➤ demographic trends for your community, including population growth;

➤ protection of heritage buildings (saved, or added to conservancy lists);

➤ library usage;

➤ return on investment (i.e. financial impact/multiplier effect of each dollar spent on arts/culture/heritage and the total economic impact it generates); and

➤ pedestrian traffic and economic activity in the downtown.

There are also some *qualitative* indicators that may be as important as other statistics, although admittedly harder to put numbers against:

➤ What are community attitudes?

➤ What is the quality of life in the municipality?

➤ Is there a sense of neighbourhood peace and security?

➤ Do you have a vibrant, growing arts community?

➤ Is there any change in perception by the local population, and by outside groups?

➤ Is the community having fun?

➤ Is there greater awareness of/support for arts, culture, and heritage?

➤ How do you stack up against your competitors?

There may also be specific, local indicators that can be identified – for example, a particular cultural site that has been saved or rejuvenated.

Indicators and benchmarks should be used carefully. Trends are more important than a particular number in a given year. It takes time to shift local attitudes, change behaviour, and influence outside opinions.

Annual or bi-annual report cards are a responsible approach. Used to indicate trends and broad statistical directions, they are more useful than arguing over a fraction of a percentage change in some particular statistic.

Branding

If there is a misunderstood, misused, and abused word in marketing today, it is probably "branding."

Canadian municipalities, provincial governments, and the federal government have spent millions – probably billions by now – to research, create, and promote their respective images/brands/logos/identity. Much of it has been a failure.

Century-old multinational billion-dollar corporations have invested enormous resources over many years, utilizing top international consultants and experts, to protect and improve their brands. So, why would anybody think a sub-committee of five earnest local councillors could develop a new municipal image?

Calling your community "The City of _____ (fill in the blank – trees, bridges, flowers, cement trucks, or whatever)" is not a brand. A cute logo or a clever slogan is not a brand. (For an insightful book on this subject, see *A logo is not a brand,* by Ted Matthews.)

Canada has writhed for years about trying to change the international perception of our country being "moose, mountains, and mounties."

Cities and countries have tried, with almost a complete lack of success, to run occasional advertising campaigns, and then are shocked with the poor results.

To return to one of the original premises of this book, what is the buzz about your community? Or, is there *any* buzz at all?

There's no use even embarking on a branding exercise until you have the product in place. That's the reason the "Creative City" concepts are so crucial – they help to create and build the kind of community that you want for the future: A Creative Community.

Cultural Planning offers the opportunity to develop a new, fresher, more contemporary and quite possibly more compelling image for your community. The City of Innovation. The County of Creativity. The Town of Ideas. The Smartest Community. The City of _____.

Or, maybe slogans don't matter any more in marketing your community … maybe the success stories and the actions are more important. Maybe the buzz created by those actions is more urgent. Maybe the text message of one Gen Xer about how cool their community is to another Gen Xer in another community is more important. Maybe media stories about how smart or cultured or caring your city is will be more important. Maybe actions to improve your community speak more loudly than paid ads. Maybe word-of-mouth about what's happening in a great community will mean more than glitzy television ads.

Municipal crests. I'm not sure many 28 year-old university grads looking to start a new high-tech global business relate to the typical Canadian municipal crest showing a dead elk, a steam locomotive, and a sheaf of grain … or whatever.

Again, a logo is not a brand. A slogan is not a marketing campaign. A hope is not an economic development strategy.

It takes absolutely huge dollars and effort to change your community's image and brand (to change it for the better, that is – a negative change can happen overnight in a media maelstrom, leaving you flattened and wondering what happened; see: SARS, Toronto). It takes a total community effort. Everyone must be focused on reinforcing and supporting the brand. It is very hard to do, and the risks of failure are very high.

Don't even try branding until you have the community positioned where you want. You're just wasting public money until the product is right. Even then, this will be a long, expensive, and exhausting process for which there is no guarantee of success. New consumer products are introduced all the time, many of which never succeed. Even if they do succeed for awhile, what's their longevity? Remember VCRs? Cassette tapes? Heck, LPs! Eighty percent of new restaurants don't last three years.

Marketing a municipality (or a country) is an enormous challenge, and one fraught with peril. Get your political enemies to sit on that sub-committee.

Development Charges

In some provinces, development charges for cultural facilities are not permitted. Utterly ridiculous. Terrible government policy. Fight to change it if you live in such a province.

Development charges are paid by developers (well, in truth by the homeowner or business purchasing or leasing the property) to pay for the added costs of new development. It goes against every reasonable and responsible principle of Cultural Planning that a portion of these charges should not be coming back to assist in the construction of cultural facilities.

For a provincial government to not understand that building the cultural infrastructure is just as important as building the physical infrastructure shows that that provincial government is incredibly out-of-touch and needing to update its policies.

This is a winnable challenge for municipalities. Go forth and fight.

Tax Policies

Both the federal and provincial governments reap substantial rewards from the hard work and investments by local municipalities to build, operate, and expand cultural, arts, sports, and heritage facilities.

The senior governments get huge revenue streams from the federal and provincial sales taxes that are added to the price of tickets to attend these events.

Municipalities get the costs; other orders of government get the revenue. This *must* change.

As a minimum, municipalities should be getting one-half of the sales tax generated from tickets to arts/cultural/sports/heritage facilities and events in their community. The money should be specifically ear-marked for investment and re-investment in these sectors.

This would provide a constant revenue stream of operating dollars to help municipalities with the costs to maintain and upgrade such facilities. No one should have illusions that museums, libraries, performing arts centres, or similar facilities are going to make money. It is a cost of providing a civilized, vibrant, and cultured community. But, for other orders of government to reap all the benefits and municipalities to be left without is unfair.

People laughed 10 years ago when municipalities began the fight to get a share of the gas tax. Today, that policy is enshrined in the budget. This can be the next winnable battle.

Attracting the "Best and Brightest" to Public Service

There are dramatic changes going on in the workplace and there is growing concern that public service is not attracting a sufficient number of the "best and brightest."

The baby boomers (those born between 1946 and 1960) are beginning to retire. Theirs was a generation of social upheaval that forced global societal changes, and they are not giving up control easily. The Gen Xrs were born between 1961 and 1981, and are tech savvy, and well-educated, with different life values. The Gen Ys were born between 1981 and 2001, and grew up with very protected and structured lives; their generation has been shaped by technology and digital media.

Many (older) municipal officials don't understand these emerging leaders. There can be a considerable disconnect between traditional ways of managing people and the needs/wants of the newer generations. Perhaps it is easiest to have them define themselves:

"Emerging leaders are a blend of Gen X and Y ... we say that Gen Y is like Gen X on steroids, with both characterized by: being change and adrenaline junkies; frequent career changes; tendency toward personal not positional authority; very well-educated, highly demanding in terms of career expectations; strong desire to be mentored; desire to find meaning in their work; work in organizations whose mission/vision they can believe in; and opportunity to participate in community development through work/professional life. What we [i.e. from the findings of the emerging leaders research] want: opportunity to contribute to community (active participation, not just "writing cheques"); opportunity to learn and be mentored; opportunity to connect with one another and current leaders to help build the community for the future; a stronger, more relevant community brand to aid in attraction/retention; greater awareness and activity around environmentalism at the community level; desire to create "new models" founded on collaboration NOT competition and silo-ing; and strongly desire an inclusive community where diversity of all kinds is supported and celebrated."
(Lindsay Sage, London's Emerging Leaders.)

In other words, there is an imminent upheaval in our workplace. Governments are in a battle to attract the best young talent, but many municipal leaders have not yet realized this fact. This is the tough question: Are we attracting the "best and brightest" into the public sector? And, specifically into municipal government?

101

The corollary is perhaps even more difficult to pose: How will we attract great future political leaders to a calling that some people see now as subjected to unrelenting media attacks, personal vilification, the inability to make positive change, a stressful family situation, personal financial penalty and public scorn? Who will choose to run for public office under those conditions?

In a world when the 2008 Canadian general election attracted only 59 percent of voters, and municipal elections routinely attract only a third of eligible voters, it is too often the young people who are not participating. This has dramatic consequences for our democratic future. It seems apparent that all three levels of government have done a mediocre job in making public service an attractive career option and opportunity.

Conclusions

These are big issues. They will not be solved by the Cultural Planning process. But, they can be identified, positions taken, and changes sought through your Cultural Plan Report and Recommendations.

The "Creative City" movement is spreading. Canadian municipalities are among the world's leaders in this movement, and we should be proud of what we are accomplishing. But, the battle is far from over. As more and more municipalities get on board with the new way of thinking and recognize the exciting possibilities and benefits that come from making culture the fourth pillar of sustainability, the strength of this movement will simply grow even more.

In the following chapter, Nancy Duxbury and her colleagues from Simon Fraser University discuss the interrelationship between culture and sustainability, and how this movement is playing out on the global stage.

The world over, this is a new way of thinking about our towns and cities, and how they can grow and prosper in the future. Canadians deserve no less than the best from their local leaders. The case studies in Chapter 14 show some good examples of such leadership in action.

Vibrant, dynamic, exciting, and contemporary communities are what people want. It is where they want to live and do business. It is up to the municipal leaders to deliver on that.

Cultural Planning is an important tool. The community engagement and the resulting recommendations are going to form the foundation for your municipality for the next few decades. It is a thrilling ride, and one that is so very important for shaping your Creative Community.

Chapter 13

Culture and Sustainable Development: A Global Perspective on Our Future

By Nancy Duxbury, Erin Schultz,
Sue Stewart, and Christina Johnson

*"Culture is not a pile of artifacts – it is us; the living, breathing sum
of us. A sustainable society depends upon a sustainable culture.
If a society's culture disintegrates, so will everything else.
Vitality is the single most important characteristic of a
sustainable culture." – Jon Hawkes, 2006*

Community development looks at communities not as simple geographical spaces, but as rich places filled with people from different social and cultural backgrounds who are constantly adapting to new environmental, economic, social, and cultural realities. Over the last decade, the importance of culture in community development – as a basis for dialogue and exchange, as a community-building catalyst for collective action and celebration, and as roots of economic competitiveness in today's creative economy – has been embraced by growing numbers of communities across Canada. Attention to culture as an integral component of our collective sustainability is now emerging.

Sustainable Development

Sustainability is fundamentally about adapting to a new ethic of living on the planet and creating a more equitable and just society through the fair distribution of social goods and resources in the world. The most commonly reported definition of sustainable development comes from the report entitled *Our Common Future*: "sustainable development is development that meets the needs of the present without compromising future generations to meet their own needs." (World Commission on Environment and Development, 1987, p. 43.)

Traditionally, sustainability has been focused on an environmental framework, and environmental concerns continue to be the cornerstone of sustainable development. As the concept has matured, increasing emphasis has been placed on its interconnection to the economic, social, and cultural dimensions of development.

Within the sustainability field, culture is often discussed in terms of cultural capital, defined as "traditions and values, heritage and place, the arts, diversity and social history." (Roseland et al., 2005, p. 12.) The stock of cultural capital, both tangible and intangible, is what we inherit from past generations, and what we will pass onto future generations. Cultural capital is seen to contribute to quality of life and better knowledge of ourselves. The limitations in this "capital" perspective are balanced by more expansive definitions of culture, such as looking at culture as the ways that "we make sense of our lives together" or, in more formal terms, as the social production of meaning. (Hawkes, 2006.)

For governments wishing to enhance their capacity to re-engage with their constituencies and to support the development of sustainable, resilient communities, applying a cultural perspective is a way to encourage all of the government's activities to positively impact on these objectives.

There is a range of specific benefits to government from the adoption of a cultural perspective within their planning processes. A cultural perspective:

▶ identifies the aspirations and values of communities as being at the foundation of society;

▶ opens a pathway for the active voices of communities to be heard;

▶ facilitates the processes used to discuss our futures, evaluate our pasts, and act in the present;

▶ provides the intellectual tools with which contemporary planning concepts can be integrated;

▶ improves the theoretical planning model;

▶ improves the capacity for public expression to affect planning processes;

▶ improves the integration of public program management. (Hawkes, 2006.)

There is a growing international movement to increase the recognition of culture in public discourses, policy, and planning regarding sustainability. UNESCO's Decade of Education for Sustainable Development (2005-2014) takes as its foundation the four-pillar definition of sustainability. The Decade is a proactive initiative toward environmental, economic, social, and cultural sustainability throughout the world, teaching individuals, institutions, and societies how to ensure improvement in quality of life today and for the future. The Agenda 21 for Culture, endorsed in Barcelona, Spain by 100 cities in 2004, is a commitment to ensure that culture is included in urban policies.

Australia: Four Pillars of Sustainability

In *The Fourth Pillar of Sustainability: Culture's Essential Role in Public Planning*, Jon Hawkes argued that in order for public planning to be more effective, government must develop a framework that evaluates the cultural impacts of environmental, economic, and social decisions and plans currently being implemented in cities and communities. With this book, Hawkes addressed the need for a cultural perspective in public planning and policy by proposing practical measures for integration.

These ideas were enthusiastically taken up by the City of Port Phillip, Australia, and were used as the basis of a framework for its city planning and policy (see City of Port Philip Corporate Plan 2002-2006). Port Phillip was the first Australian local government to formally incorporate cultural vitality, and give it equal status alongside the other traditional triple bottom line considerations (economic, social, and environmental).

New Zealand: Four Well-beings of Community Sustainability

In 2006, New Zealand's Ministry for Culture and Heritage created a well-being model that includes cultural, environmental, social, and economic dimensions. The model was created in response to the *Local Government Act, 2002* (section 10), which states that local government is responsible for promoting "the social, economic, environmental, and cultural well-being of communities, in the present and for the future" (New Zealand Ministry for Culture and Heritage, 2006, p. 1.) Through this model, the ministry emphasizes the necessity for councils to deal with all four types of well-being in order to achieve sustainable development.

Cultural well-being is defined as the vitality, enjoyed by communities and individuals, arising from "participation in recreation, creative, and cultural activities; and the freedom to retain, interpret and express their arts, history, heritage, and traditions." (New Zealand's Ministry for Culture and Heritage, 2006.)

Canada: A Medicine Wheel Approach to Community Quality of Life

Recent work to develop indicators to explore and document the quality of life among Aboriginal people living in the Greater Vancouver region – Nathan Cardinal and Emilie Adin's *An Urban Aboriginal Life* (2005) – used a medicine wheel as a framework to determine categories of indicators. As shown in Figure 1 below, the medicine wheel depicts four traditional directions: north (environmental), south (social), west (economic), and east (cultural). The cultural component included indicators relating to the vibrancy and prevalence of participation in traditional activities, and the speaking of traditional languages.

Four key segments of Aboriginal society – male, female, children and youth, and adults and elders – crosscut the four elements. These four segments represent different groups and viewpoints in Aboriginal society. Each of these segments is considered to be critical to give context to the Aboriginal community's overall well-being. A holistic and flexible planning and development process surrounds the medicine wheel, guiding the framework's development, maintenance, and evolution.

Figure 1. Canada: Medicine Wheel Framework for *An Urban Aboriginal Life*

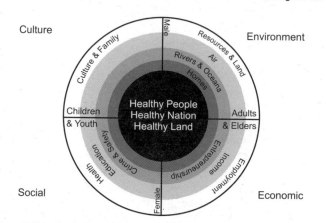

Source: Nathan Cardinal & Emilie Adin, *An Urban Aboriginal Life: The 2005 Indicators Report on the Quality of Life of Aboriginal People in the Greater Vancouver Region*, Centre for Native Policy and Research, 2005

West Indies: Culture as the Fourth and Central Pillar

From the perspective of developing countries, and especially Small Island Developing States (SIDS), Keith Nurse (2006) developed a four-pillar model of sustainable development in which culture is presented as the fourth and central pillar of the sustainable development framework, fully integrated into that of the other pillars of the economy, the social, and the ecological. This model is based in a view of the sustainable development paradigm as part of the growth of new social movements and a rising wave of discontent with conventional development theory and practice. The model places an emphasis on cultural diversity as an equivalent to genetic diversity in the sustainable development debate.

This approach to sustainable development prioritizes the following values:

► cultural identity (the social unit of development is a culturally defined community, and the development of this community is rooted in the specific values and institutions of this culture);

► self-reliance (each community relies primarily on its own strength and resources);

► social justice (the development effort should give priority to those most in need);

► ecological balance (the resources of the biosphere are utilized in full awareness of the potential of local ecosystems, as well as the global and local limits imposed on present and future generations). (Friberg and Hettne, 1985, p. 220; cited in Nurse, 2006, p. 38.)

Within this framework, the cultural sector (i.e. the arts sector and cultural industries) is viewed as playing a dual role: both an arena for identity formation and an economic sector with growth potential and a key driver of the "digital and intellectual property economy." Cultural industries are identified as a "critical strategic resource in the move towards creating sustainable development options in SIDS."

A Canadian Application: ICSPs

An Integrated Community Sustainability Plan (ICSP) can be defined as "a long-term plan, developed in consultation with community members, that provides direction for the community to realize sustainability objectives it has for the environmental, cultural, social, and economic dimensions of its identity." (Nanda, 2007.) As the Alberta Urban Municipalities Association (2006) has put it, municipal sustainability planning is an opportunity for municipalities to proactively move towards a sustainable future, "one where a strong economy and participative governance models protect ecological integrity, and contribute to a vibrant cultural scene and strong social cohesion."

An ICSP:

► respects and builds on existing planning approaches;

► enhances community involvement in the planning process, including those who do not traditionally participate;

► requires the inclusion of a cultural dimension (along with the traditional elements of sustainable development – economic, environmental, and social);

► involves long-term planning (20 years and beyond); and

► encourages inter-municipal collaborations to plan regionally (for entire areas that correspond to economic, socio-demographic, ecological and cultural realities) and can lead to synergies. (Nanda, 2007.)

An ICSP is meant to be a true "umbrella plan" that "moves the planning bar forward" – a long-term vision and strategic framework ensuring that all decision-making and planning processes are coordinated and work towards desired outcomes. An ICSP differs from an Official Community Plan in three ways: (1) it usually has a longer-range focus than an OCP (up to 30 years); (2) it is generally more holistic; and (3) an ICSP has an emphasis on infrastructure rather than land use, with consideration of sustainability principles paramount.

ICSPs were required of municipalities by the gas tax fund agreements signed in 2005-2006 with the provinces and territories, but not universally (Saskatchewan and Quebec were exempted from this requirement). The agreements allow recipients to use a portion of gas tax funds to develop increased local capacity to undertake community-based planning. The agreements do not require ICSPs to be submitted for federal approval, but Infrastructure Canada has an enabling role, largely through the Gas Tax Fund Oversight Committees in each jurisdiction. Although ICSP requirements vary from jurisdiction to jurisdiction, all ICSPs must follow the "four pillar" approach to sustainability (environment, economic, social, cultural sustainability). (Ostry, 2008.)

Since the gas tax fund agreements differ from province to province or territory, it has largely been left up to each jurisdiction to develop materials and guidebooks on ICSPs for use by municipalities. Often, the task has been taken up by the provincial association of municipalities, at times in parallel to efforts of the provincial municipal relations department.

Some provinces/territories are advising their municipalities to draw on pre-existing plans and strategies to formulate their ICSP, notably Nunavut and Ontario. The BC guides mention the *CCP Handbook: A Guide to Comprehensive Community Planning for First Nations in British Columbia*, created by Indian and Northern Affairs Canada for BC. The federal government, besides providing GTF funding, is facilitating research, sharing of information, and general support/advice during the development of frameworks and guidelines (see Infrastructure Canada, 2008).

At the time of writing (Fall 2008), few communities have completed ICSPs, but many are in the process of doing so. The deadline for the development of ICSPs is January 31, 2010, although some provinces have established earlier deadlines (for example, Nova Scotia requires ICSPs to be completed by September 2009). The Province of Ontario has taken the position that the existing legislative framework is sustainable in nature, and there is no need for new plans to be developed, so ICSPs may not be as widely developed in that province. However, recent and rising attention to Cultural Planning in Ontario municipalities may fuel a more long-term, integrated approach to community planning and sustainability issues, framed by the four-pillar approach to sustainable development.

With so few ICSPs completed across the country at this time, it is difficult to assess the extent to which cultural considerations are/will be integrated meaningfully in the ICSPs. Most of the plans accessible today have paid some attention to cultural considerations. For the most part, culture is considered separately from other dimensions of sustainability in the currently completed ICSPs. Where attention is given to culture, the emphasis is on:

► future development being sensitive to the cultural identity of the community;

► the importance of retaining traditional languages and heritage;

► the preservation of heritage buildings;

► increasing support (funding) for arts and culture;

► equitable access to arts and cultural activities independent of socio-economic status; and

► recognizing the economic value of arts and culture.

Conclusion

As reflected in the definitions and perspectives presented at the beginning of this chapter, the scope and potential of the cultural dimension of sustainable development is broad and powerful. In comparison, some approaches to ICSPs appear to only "skim the surface" of the potential inherent in fully thinking through this aspect of the community and its development into the future. Cultural continuity, adaptation, evolution, and intercultural dialogue – necessarily rooted in diverse and open exchanges and broad participation – are key elements to address and negotiate challenges, opportunities, and change, and to carry our collective knowledge and experiences into the future in meaningful ways.

The ICSP framework is pushing Canada to the forefront of countries holistically embracing the four-pillar model of sustainable development. The holistic visions and strategies resulting from the process of developing ICSPs have the potential to help guide our communities' futures in balanced and meaningful ways.

The prevailing challenges are three-fold. The first challenge is to fully think through and embrace the potential of the cultural pillar (broadly defined) in a rich, meaningful, and important manner that links it to the other three dimensions in many ways. The second challenge is to foster and maintain a truly integrative perspective, so that the environmental, economic, social, and cultural lenses are brought to bear in all policy, planning, assessment, implementation, monitoring, and other processes of a community. The third challenge is one of implementation – to take the vision into reality, ensuring that the holistic perspective is reflected in action and is embedded in continued community involvement.

The origins of this chapter are found in a working paper of the Centre of Expertise on Culture and Communities (CECC), Simon Fraser University, entitled "Culture as a Key Dimension of Sustainability: Exploring Concepts, Themes, and Models." (Duxbury & Gillette, 2007.) This paper formed the basis for the Creative City Network of Canada's Creative City News: Special Edition 4: "Exploring the Cultural Dimensions of Sustainability," 2007. Under the auspices of the CECC, Erin Schultz, Sue Stewart, and Lidia Varbanova have conducted additional research on international developments, trends, and models, which also informs this chapter. For further information, see: <www.cultureandcommunities.ca>.

Chapter 14

Case Studies

Author's Note: Cultural Planning is being used successfully in municipalities of all sizes in Canada. These case studies of four very different Canadian communities outline clearly their process and results, and how every community will adapt and shape its own Cultural Plan and process according to its own particular needs. The first two cases are authored by Greg Baeker, and the third and fourth were contributed by Nancy Duxbury et al. — *Gord Hume*

CASE #1: Small Rural – Prince Edward County, Ontario

Prince Edward County is a rural municipality situated in Eastern Ontario with a population of 25,000 people. A 250,000 acre isthmus that juts 40 kilometres south into Lake Ontario, the county boasts some 800 kilometres of shore framed by the lake and the Bay of Quinte, due south of Belleville. "The County," as it is affectionately known, is a two-hour drive east of Toronto, 2½ hour drive southwest of Ottawa, and a 3½ hour drive west of Montreal. The United States border to upper New York State is a 1½ hour drive at the eastern edge of Lake Ontario at Gananoque.

Like many rural areas in Canada, Prince Edward County faces enormous challenges related to economic restructuring. Traditional dependencies on agriculture and a relatively small number of industries leave many areas vulnerable. In the context of the larger challenge facing Ontario's industrial base, many communities face very real questions of viability in the face of increased unemployment, a reduced tax base, and the reduced capacity to pay for basic services and infrastructure.

Prince Edward County is emerging as a leading region in Ontario and nationally in developing a "new rural economy" based on creativity and quality of place.

In 2004, an economic development strategy concluded the county would never be competitive using traditional economic development strategies "chasing business and industry." However, it could build a sustainable economic future through a strategy rooted in quality of place and creativity. The strategy identified four "pillars" – culture, tourism, agriculture, and commerce/industry – for focused development.

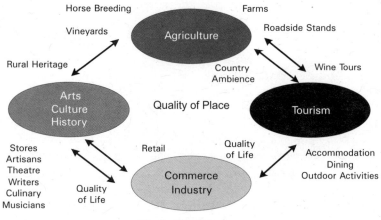

Horse Breeding · Farms

Vineyards · Agriculture · Roadside Stands

Rural Heritage · Country Ambience · Wine Tours

Arts Culture History · Quality of Place · Tourism

Stores Artisans Theatre Writers Culinary Musicians · Retail · Quality of Life · Accommodation Dining Outdoor Activities

Quality of Life · Commerce Industry

Wineries Retail Estate

How was the Cultural Plan developed?

In 2005, a Cultural Strategic Plan was undertaken. More than 300 county residents participated in the plan through surveys, interviews, and public meetings.

A major conclusion of the planning process was that one of the most serious barriers to change and to better integrating culture in economic and community development was a limited vision or mindset about what culture was and its importance in the county. As a result, the plan draws attention to the following:

➤ more than 300 cultural resources and related tourism and hospitality organizations exist in the county;

➤ employment in the information/culture/entertainment sector combined with accommodation and food now exceeds forestry and agriculture;

➤ the county is ideally situated to capitalize on a rapidly expanding market for cultural and culinary tourism, drawing on a catchment area that includes Montreal, Ottawa, Toronto, and several highly populated northern US states;

➤ the number of tourism visits has increased 74 percent from 253,000 in 1999 to 440,000 in 2004; and

➤ the amount of visitor spending has increased by 168 percent from $24 million in 1999 to $65 million in 2004.

"Leveraging Growth and Managing Change: A Cultural Plan for Prince Edward County" was completed in 2005. In 2006, the plan was awarded best economic development strategic plan by the Economic Development Council of Ontario.

The plan begins with the following vision statement.

> We are all settlers in Prince Edward County. For over 200 years, people have chosen to come to this island, to create a life for themselves and their families, and in the process to build a unique and remarkable county culture.
>
> Our culture is a product of this beautiful place and the energy and passion of the many generations who settled here. It is the glue that connects old and new residents, our past and our future. It is where our history and creativity meet.

The plan also identified the following defining characteristics of county culture.

➤ our unique island character, scenic shorelines, sandbanks, and maritime history;

➤ our proud Loyalist traditions and history;

➤ our rural landscapes, family farms, and proud agricultural heritage;

➤ our many villages, hamlets, and small town ambience;

➤ our historic homes, farmsteads, and heritage streetscapes;

➤ our long history and renown for agriculture and food production – from barley to canning, to dairy and cheese, to grapes and wine;

➤ our entrepreneurial spirit and capacity to renew and reinvent our economy;

➤ our writers, visual and performing artists, and their creative excellence; and

➤ our sense of community – one that connects old and new residents.

The plan established three mechanisms to support collaboration and shared planning and decision making:

Cultural Roundtable – a cross-sectoral strategic leadership group.

Cultural "rally" – an annual opportunity for the larger community to celebrate achievements and identify new opportunities.

Community forums – ongoing events to support networking and community dialogue.

The plan defined a multi-year agenda, in two parts. For each of the bulleted themes below, specific short-, medium- and long-term actions were identified.

A. Capacity Building for Culture

► planning and policy;

► sectoral planning and priority setting;

► integration with county plans;

► investment and resource development;

► capital investments;

► organizational investments;

► project funding;

► capacity building;

► partnerships and collaboration;

► research and information;

► training and leadership development; and

► marketing and audience development.

B. County Strategic Priorities

Managing growth – taking steps to ensure needed growth and development does not undermine quality of place. Includes:

► managing growth and development in Picton; and

► managing growth and development across the county.

Cultural places and spaces – extending and improving the places where culture happens in the county. Includes:

► promote an integrated vision of cultural places in the county ("Hub and Spokes"); and

► improve and extend access to cultural venues – spaces and facilities – across the county.

Cultural tourism – build on existing strengths and overcome barriers to collaboration.

Extend the season – build shoulder seasons through programming.

Strengthen tourism packaging – based on an interpretive framework for the county. Exploit strong links (cluster) of cultural, eco, and culinary tourism.

Strengthen marketing and promotion – through collaboration and shared investment.

CASE #2: Mid-Size – Saskatoon, Saskatchewan

Creative Connections: Building Our "Creative City" was an anchor project in Saskatoon's designation as a Cultural Capital of Canada in 2006. It was envisioned as a legacy project, one intended to have a long-term impact on the city. The purpose of the project was to build Saskatoon's capacity to realize its potential as a "Creative City."

The project did not complete a full Cultural Plan, but did put in place three new "systems" built on Cultural Planning principles.

Cultural Mapping – to build a system for identifying and building a shared base of knowledge of Saskatoon's rich creative and cultural resources.

Cultural governance – to create a shared planning and decision-making (governance) mechanism connecting government, business, community, and university interests.

Networking and engagement – to strengthen communication and collaboration across the community in support of creativity and culture.

Creative Connections began as a partnership between the City of Saskatoon, the University of Saskatchewan, and the Saskatchewan Arts Board. A Cultural Roundtable chaired by University of Saskatchewan President Peter McKinnon led the project.

In addition to the three project partners, members included representatives from Tourism Saskatoon, three downtown business improvement districts (Broadway, Riversdale, and Downtown), a representative of First Nations, Saskatoon public schools, the Saskatoon police service and, of course, representatives from the creative and cultural sector in Saskatoon.

Cultural Mapping

A working group was struck to lead resource mapping. Its members included: the City of Saskatoon, University of Saskatchewan, Saskatchewan Arts Board, Tourism Saskatoon, the Broadway, Downtown and

115

Riversdale Business Improvement Districts, Saskculture (Saskatchewan's lottery supported funding agency serving for arts, heritage, multiculturalism and creative industries), and the Meewasin Conservation Authority (a conservation agency responsible for preserving the river basin of the Saskatchewan River, itself a partnership of the City of Saskatoon, the University of Saskatchewan, and the provincial government).

Early on, the city's planning department agreed to provide the GIS platform on which to build the mapping system, and to support the ongoing management of this system with the understanding that responsibility for populating, updating and continually enriching information would be a shared responsibility among a range of community and business partners.

In Saskatoon, mapping the community identity involved two steps.

Community-wide survey – A web-based survey was widely distributed in the community through the networks (and email distribution lists) of Roundtable members and other organizations. Recipients were invited to reflect on and identify the symbols, stories, qualities of place, etc. that made Saskatoon unique for them. They were also asked to look ahead, to imagine Saskatoon as a vibrant, successful "Creative City" in 20 years, and to describe that place. Survey responses were then reviewed and synthesized into recurring themes and narratives.

Community forums – A series of forums were then held with specific community groups. These included: youth (two Grade 8 classes and a summer youth program), First Nations, and a specific neighbourhood that was serving as the site of an artist in the community project (another Cultural Capitals project). Participants were invited to identify their own place-based stories and specific places in the city that had particular meaning for them. These stories were posted to an oversize map of the city generated by the planning department. All input was recorded in a variety of formats, and will eventually be accessible as part of a web-based cultural map of Saskatoon.

There was no expectation that Creative Connections would generate a definitive picture of the city's identity. Rather, the goal was to demonstrate "proof of concept" for a process that will be ongoing.

Identity mapping has practical and powerful applications in marketing and promoting a community. Two other Cultural Capital projects were a cultural tourism strategy for Saskatoon and Tourism Saskatoon, and Crescent – a culture-based marketing and development strategy involving the three downtown business improvement districts. Both pointed to the authentic cultural experience of Saskatoon as the city's primary asset. Identity mapping can inform, enhance, and help to market these experiences. Results can form the basis of tours, itineraries, and other tourism products.

Cultural Governance

The second goal of Creative Connections was to establish an ongoing governance mechanism to support cross-sectoral collaboration. Through a process of research and discussion, including examining examples of cultural governance systems in other communities, a governance system was proposed with three components:

Roundtable – This cross-sectoral leadership group is responsible for building shared vision, continuously identifying strategic opportunities, and mobilizing public and private sector resources.

Working groups – Task-driven groups struck by the Roundtable tackle specific opportunities, drawing expertise from the institutions or constituencies represented on the Roundtable, and more broadly in the community.

Vehicles for broader community engagement – To ensure the governance mechanism remains fed by broader community input and ideas, vehicles such as community forums on specific issues and annual community summits are needed to round out the governance system.

What is the Roundtable's mission and guiding objectives?

The Roundtable defined the following framework of mission, roles, and principles.

Mission

The Creative City Roundtable works to support Saskatoon to realize its potential as a "Creative City" through leadership, innovation, and action.

Roles

It will realize this mission by adopting the following roles:

▶   to bring together champions dedicated to creativity and culture;

▶   to articulate and promote a shared vision of the importance of creativity and culture in Saskatoon;

▶   to mobilize knowledge by linking researchers, policy makers, and practitioners;

117

► to advocate and support the integration of culture in policies, plans, and investments within the municipality and across all sectors; and

► to enable action on issues identified by the Roundtable or the community.

Guiding Principles

Sustainability – a holistic view of city building based on "four pillars" or dimensions of sustainability – economic prosperity, social equity, environmental sustainability, and cultural vitality.

Inclusive engagement, partnerships, and collaboration – inclusive engagement and collaboration across the community.

Emergence and purpose – balancing a commitment to open-ended dialogue that generates new understandings while advancing concrete plans and actions.

Evidence-based decision making – decision making across all sectors, based on sound information and assessments of outcomes.

Who will form the membership of the Roundtable?

The group defined the criterion for inclusion on the Roundtable as follows:

> Successful cultural governance requires the engagement of passionate, knowledgeable individuals across all sectors committed to creativity and culture as essential to building sustainable cities and communities. Not all of the following sectors will be involved at all times. It is expected that Roundtable membership will evolve organically in response to interest and need. Members will include leaders drawn from:
>
> • creative and cultural sector;
>
> • municipal council and staff;
>
> • business community;
>
> • community sectors; and
>
> • educational institutions, school boards, and post-secondary institutions.

CASE #3: First Nations – Teslin Tlingit Council and Village of Teslin, Yukon

Teslin is a century-old townsite located on the Alaska Highway that grew up from a trading post in the early 1900s to a community of about 450. Like most Yukon communities, Teslin is home to a First Nation that has lived in the area for centuries – the Teslin Tlingit Council, or Dakh-ka Tlingit, an inland Tlingit group that migrated through the Taku River from the Alaskan Coast. The Tlingit people relied on this area for subsistence and cultural identity long before it became a stop over for prospectors.

As a testament to the very strong relationship between the Village of Teslin and the Teslin Tlingit Council, a decision was made to collaborate on one common plan for the whole community. A joint planning committee made up of appointees of each local government, as well as members of the public was established.

The planning committee conducted interviews with members of the public, made a presentation to the school, asked youth for their input on the plan, and conducted a review of existing planning documents to ensure previous consultative processes were considered.

Both the municipal council and the Teslin Tlingit Executive Council were involved at each step of the planning. Public meetings were held in March and September of 2007 to ensure that residents had an opportunity to express their views.

The resulting Integrated Community Sustainability Plan contains the overarching vision, values, and goals of the community. It also contains the initial sustainability analysis and priorities for the basic infrastructure that governments provide to the citizens. The committee will continue planning for other priority areas as they strive to meet the needs and expectations of the residents of Teslin, while moving the community closer towards sustainability.

Teslin Vision Statement

Teslin will be a community that provides for the long-term social, cultural and economic needs of its residents while protecting and respecting the natural environment that sustains them.

Values

The Community of Teslin will develop a long-term community sustainability plan based on the values of its residents. Goals must reflect these values. While recognizing that individual residents have diverse personal values and goals, they believe that the residents of Teslin share the following community values:

➤ respect for our neighbours, our community, and ourselves;

➤ the health of our residents;

➤ knowledge, learning, and education;

➤ our Tlingit heritage and culture; and

➤ the natural environment that sustains our community.

(Cultural) Goal – The protection and preservation of the Tlingit culture, heritage, and language.

Our community's identity is linked to and, in some ways, dependent on the Tlingit culture, heritage, and language. It is in the interest of all citizens to know and understand the culture, to respect the heritage, and to encourage the use of and preservation of the language.

Description of Success

In a sustainable Teslin, the Teslin Tlingit Council have succeeded in preserving the Tlingit language by passing a Language Act and implementing a traditional knowledge framework, which together bring the language into the every day activities of government.

A complete heritage and language strategy, combined with the strong focus on language usage, has created a strong, nurturing environment for the preservation and cultivation of the Tlingit culture, heritage, and language.

In concrete terms, every Tlingit citizen is fluent in the language and there is a strong interest among non-citizens in the culture and heritage and how it can contribute to community life as a whole.

Through this shared respect, the community has been able to work together to preserve and protect known heritage buildings, sites, and trails, while ensuring any development respects these heritage resources. Adding to the economic sustainability of the community, there is a growing market for traditional crafts and cultural performances.

We are a community that values our Tlingit past, and we have ensured that it remains an integral part of our community into the future.

CASE #4: Whistler, British Columbia

Dr. Karl-Henrik Robert, founder of The Natural Step, first visited Whistler in 2000 for a snowboard holiday, and gave a few talks about the TNS framework. Whistler had always been proactive around the environment, yet had never developed a formal definition of, or framework for, sustainability. An early adopter program was formed, which included the Resort Municipality of Whistler, Whistler Blackcomb, the Fairmont Chateau Whistler, Tourism Whistler, One-Hour Photo, and AWARE (Association of Whistler Area Residents for the Environment). The early adopter organizations developed sustainability programs within their own organizations and supported the broader rollout to the rest of the community. As a result, "Whistler: It's Our Nature" was developed as a community outreach program to help educate and inspire around sustainability.

The community soon decided that it wanted to develop a comprehensive and long-term vision, plan, and process rooted in sustainability. A program called "Whistler: It's Our Future" was developed, again to understand community members' hopes and priorities for the future. The result is Whistler2020, the first comprehensive sustainability plan in North America to use the science-based TNS framework at all levels of development and implementation.

About Whistler2020

Rooted in community values and a science-based approach to sustainability, Whistler2020 is long-term, comprehensive, community-developed, community-implemented, and action-focused. The process ensures that Whistler2020 is a "living" plan, that it drives ongoing progress, and that it is continually informed by interested community members.

Building on the previous five-year vision, Whistler2020 was developed in four phases over three years of consultation and community collaboration before it was adopted in 2005. During Phase 1, "success factors" were identified. In Phase 2, five alternative futures were explored and assessed by the community. Phase 3 involved crafting a preferred future and developing the draft plan with the involvement of 16 community task forces. In Phase 4, the preferred future was transformed into the Whistler2020 vision, and the 16 strategies were completed with ongoing action-planning by the strategy task forces and on-the-ground implementation through the involvement and commitment of a broad spectrum of implementing organizations throughout the community.

The Regional Municipality of Whistler houses the Whistler2020 Team, but the creativity, direction, and execution of the plan are products of the ongoing dedication and commitment of Whistler2020 partners, community task forces, and many organizations and businesses.

Arts, Cultural, and Heritage Strategy

… Culture is made up of a society's beliefs, values, and heritage, and has many components, including performing, literary, visual arts, heritage buildings, and biographies. This strategy addresses all expressions of culture and explores opportunities for building a flourishing arts, cultural, and heritage scene in Whistler. First Nations are an important component of this strategy and integrated throughout.

Description of Success

In 2020, Whistler is renowned for world-class arts, cultural, and heritage opportunities that have become a part of Whistler's spirit and community life. They are creative, authentic, diverse, sustainable, accessible, and affordable to both residents and visitors. By this time:

▶ The community is passionate about arts, culture, and heritage, which have become a part of Whistler's spirit and community life, and alive with creative energy and aesthetic appreciation.

▶ A range of authentic and creative arts, cultural, and heritage opportunities are meaningful, accessible, and financially affordable to residents and visitors.

▶ Arts, cultural, and heritage opportunities attract visitors and contribute to the experience and local economy.

▶ Whistler's people and history, the natural environment, and First Nations culture are retained, celebrated, and reflected through authentic and diverse offerings.

▶ Local and regional heritage, culture, and community spirit are shared locally and beyond Whistler.

▶ Arts, culture, and heritage, and their local creators and contributors, are appreciated and supported as cornerstones of the resort community's health, vitality, and economic prosperity.

▶ Whistler is renowned for world-class arts, cultural, and heritage opportunities, and has become a magnet for international artists who come here to perform, create, teach, and be inspired.

▶ There is a physical and organizational focal point for the diversity of arts, culture, and heritage activities that spread throughout the community.

▶ Ecologically harmful substances and practices are replaced with more sustainable alternatives.

Ideas for More Information, Funding, and Help

1. Check with your provincial government's Cultural Ministry – there may be information, background, examples from that province's municipalities, even funding opportunities for local projects on the ministry's website.

2. Also check with the local/provincial Arts Council(s). These are natural allies with "Creative City" initiatives, and offer links and partnerships as well as local contacts and support.

3. Libraries are a wonderful source of information and expertise. With web links and search engines local librarians can help you find wonderful examples of Cultural Planning from around the world.

4. Most provinces fund arts and cultural programs through, for example, lottery and/or gaming revenues; check with provincial funders such as the Ontario Trillium Foundation for financial assistance.

5. The Government of Canada has recently made Cultural Mapping a municipal program that can receive significant federal funding. At the time of writing, this program was funded by the Department of Canadian Heritage, which has regional offices across Canada.

6. Business for the Arts is a Toronto-based organization that provides support and assistance to municipalities and arts organizations by offering business partnerships and providing matching fund grants.

Interesting Web Connections

Artscape's Creative Clusters Development program: This program builds the capacity of Canadian Communities in developing and managing projects in the creative, arts and cultural sectors <www.torontoartscape.on.ca/>.

Canada Council for the Arts <www.canadacouncil.ca>.

Canadian Heritage ministry: A number of federal programs including Cultural Capitals, Cultural Spaces, and other federal programs <www.pch.gc.ca/ pc-ch>.

Communities in Bloom: A national program to support communities across Canada that are beautifying their municipalities, building pride and enhancing quality of life locally <www.communitiesinbloom.ca>.

Creative City Network of Canada: A network of municipal staffers involved with Cultural Planning. CCNC has done valuable seminars across Canada and provides good information <www.creativecity.ca>.

Environment Canada Eco Action Fund: A federal program to encourage local action to protect, rehabilitate, or enhance the natural environment <www.ec.gc.ca>.

International Downtowns Association: An international organization supporting culture as a critical element in the renewal and rejuvenation of downtowns, and creating a sense of place <www.ida-downtown.org/eweb/startpage.aspx>.

Canadian Green Buildings Council <www.cagbc.ca>.

City of Vancouver: Public art program and other creative city planning and community initiatives <www.vancouver.ca>.

Creative City Task Force report (original version), Creative City Committee and other municipal initiatives: then follow the links under "Creative City" <www.london.ca>.

Public Art Policy, Winnipeg Arts Council, film and television, and city of Winnipeg arts and cultural links <www.winnipeg.ca/interhom>.

Ontario Municipal Cultural Planning Partnership: An innovative amalgam of seven Ontario government ministries, municipalities, the arts and cultural sector and private businesses <www.ontariomcp.ca>.

References

Agenda 21 for Culture (2004). Developed by United Cities and Local Governments – Working Group on Culture <www.agenda21culture.net>.

Alberta Urban Municipalities Association (June 2006). *Comprehensive Guide for Municipal Sustainability Planning* <http://msp.auma.ca/digitalAssets/0/249_MSP_CompleteGuidebook_June06.pdf>.

Cardinal, Nathan and Emilie Adin (2005). *An Urban Aboriginal Life: The 2005 Indicators Report on the Quality of Life of Aboriginal People in the Greater Vancouver Region*. Vancouver: Centre for Native Policy and Research.

CCP Handbook: A Guide to Comprehensive Community Planning for First Nations in British Columbia. (August 2006). Developed by Indian and Northern Affairs in partnership with five First Nations in BC. <www.ainc-inac.gc.ca/bc/proser/fna/ccp/ccphb/ ccphb_e.html>.

City of Port Philip (2008). What is cultural vitality? City of Port Philip website <www.portphillip.vic.gov.au/what_is_cultural_vitality.html>.

Conference Board of Canada (July 2008). Valuing Culture: Measuring and Understanding Canada's Creative Economy <http://sso.conferenceboard.ca/e-Library/Document.asp?DID=2671>.

Duxbury, Nancy and Eileen Gillette (February 2007). "Culture as a key dimension of sustainability: Exploring concepts, themes, and models." Working Paper. Vancouver: Centre of Expertise on Culture and Communities, Creative City Network of Canada/Simon Fraser University.

Duxbury, Nancy, Eileen Gillette, and Kaija Pepper (May 2007). "Exploring the Cultural Dimensions of Sustainability." *Creative City News: Special Edition 4*. Vancouver: Creative City Network of Canada.

Florida, Richard (2003). *The Rise of the Creative Class: And How It's Transforming Work, Leisure, Community and Everyday Life*. New York: Basic Books. Also <www.creativeclass.com>.

Friberg, Mats and Bjorn Hettne (1985). "Greening of the World – Towards a Non-Deterministic Model of Global Processes." In Herb Addo, ed. *Development as Social Transformation*. London: Hodder and Stoughton: 204-270.

Grogan, David, Colin Mercer, and David Engwicht (1995). *Cultural Planning Handbook*, Allen & Unwin.

Hawkes, Jon (2001). *The fourth pillar of sustainability: Culture's essential role in public planning*. Commissioned by the Cultural Development Network, Victoria. Melbourne: Common Ground Publishing.

Hawkes, Jon (October 25, 2006). Creative democracy. Keynote address at Interacció '06: Community Cultural Policies, Barcelona Provincial Council, Barcelona.

Infrastructure Canada (2008). Resource Centre: Sustainable Community Planning and Development <www.infrastructure.gc.ca/links-liens/resources-ressources/resources-ressources-eng.html>.

Municipal Cultural Planning Partnership. MCPP is a coalition of agencies in Ontario working to support municipalities across the province to develop Municipal Cultural Plans. Members include seven provincial ministries (Culture; Municipal Affairs and Housing; Economic Development and Trade; Tourism; Citizenship; Agricultural and Rural Affairs; and Northern Development and Mines), the Association of Municipalities of Ontario, and business, cultural, and community agencies, as well as leading municipalities.

Nanda, Kris (October 13, 2007). Presentation delivered to Creative City Network of Canada Conference, Edmonton.

New Zealand Ministry for Culture and Heritage (2006). Cultural well-being and local government. Report 1: Definition and context of cultural well-being. Wellington, NZ: New Zealand Ministry for Culture and Heritage.

Nurse, Keith (June 2006). "Culture as the Fourth Pillar of Sustainable Development." Paper prepared for Commonwealth Secretariat, London, UK <www.fao.org/sard/common/ecg/2700/en/Cultureas4thPillarSD.pdf>.

Ostry, Adam (February 14, 2008). Presentation at FCM Sustainable Communities Conference, Ottawa.

Regional Municipality of Whistler (2005). Whistler 2020 – Arts, Culture and Heritage <www.whistler2020.ca/whistler/site/strategy.acds?context=1930599&instanceid=1930600>.

Roseland, Mark, with Sean Connelly, David Hendrickson, Chris Lindberg, and Michael Lithgow (2005). *Towards sustainable communities: Resources for citizens and their governments.* (Rev. ed.). Gabriola Island, BC: New Society Publishers.

Teslin Tlingit Council and Village of Teslin (2007). Our Bridge to the Future – Teslin Integrated Community Sustainability Plan.

Verwijnen, Jan and Panu Lehovuori (editors) (2002). *Creative Cities: Cultural Industries, Urban Development and the Information Society.* Helsinki: University of Art and Design.

World Commission on Environment and Development (1987). Our common future. Oxford & New York: Oxford University Press.

About the Contributors

Gord Hume is serving his fourth consecutive term on City Council in London, Ontario. He chaired the city's Creative City Task Force in 2004 that produced the nationally-respected report that has since guided London in adopting and implementing the recommendations. He now chairs London's Creative City Committee.

Gord is also the Chair of the Ontario Municipal Cultural Planning Partnership, a unique conglomeration of seven provincial government ministries, creative municipalities, and leading arts, cultural, and business organizations. MCPP is a resource to assist municipalities and the provincial government on Creative City concepts and adapting Municipal Cultural Planning into decision making at the local level.

Gord Hume has a fascinating background, spending 40 years in the media business and local government. He managed major radio stations, co-founded what became Canada's largest independent community newspaper, produced three record albums, founded Symphonia Canada, wrote and produced many radio and television programs, earned a bunch of major awards, and has been active in many other aspects of creative life in Canada.

Glen Murray is the chief executive officer and president of the Canadian Urban Institute. As the former Mayor of Winnipeg for six years, his vision for urban centers is anchored in practical and very successful experience on the council floor, working with business and union leaders, and collaborating with other levels of government. His vision for a new deal for cities started with the formation of the C5 – a coalition of mayors from five Canadian cities. It was during that time that he became the first chair of the Big City Mayors Caucus 2002.

He was appointed by the Prime Minister of Canada to the chair of the National Round Table on the Environment and the Economy, where his extensive experience in municipal government is helping to shape environmental policy and respond to climate change in Canada.

Dr. Greg Baeker is a regular contributor to Municipal World. He is Senior Consultant with AuthentiCity, the urban policy practice of Navigator Ltd. Greg is a nationally recognized leader in creative city building and municipal cultural planning. His work includes cultural plans and strategies for major urban centres and small rural communities.

Greg is co-author with Glen Murray and Pauline Couture of the Creative City Planning Framework, written for the City Toronto. His Cultural Strategic Plan for Prince Edward County in Ontario was awarded best strategic economic plan from the Economic Development Council of Ontario in 2006. He has completed work in Saint John, New Brunswick and Saskatoon. In Ontario his work includes plans for Chatham-Kent, Orillia, Oxford County, Sarnia-Lambton, Oakville, Hamilton, Mississauga, and the Region of Niagara.

Greg has served in senior leadership positions in the cultural sector in Canada as Executive Director of the Ontario Museum Association, Executive Coordinator of the Ontario Heritage Policy Review for the Government of Ontario - the first cross-government policy in Canada, and Professor of Arts Management at the University of Toronto. As a consultant he has completed more than 70 projects for clients in Canada and internationally.

Tim Jones is President and CEO of Artscape, <www.torontoartscape.on.ca> committed to building a world that engages art, culture and creativity as catalysts for community transformation, sustainability, prosperity and livability. Under Tim's direction since 1998, Artscape has grown from a Toronto-based affordable space provider into an international leader in culture-led regeneration and city-building through the arts.

Some of the major achievements at Artscape have included: brokering a win-win-win deal between a developer, community activists, artists and the City of Toronto to overcome a bitter development dispute in the Queen West Triangle; pioneering a new self-financing model of affordable artist live/work space; helping envision and raise the funds for $20 million Artscape Wychwood Barns – a multi-dimensional arts and environmental project at the site of the former TTC Wychwood Barns; and played a catalytic role in the development of the revitalization of the Distillery Historic District, West Queen West, and Liberty Village.

In 2008, Artscape will work on 25 projects, programs and strategies in Canada and abroad that aim to unlock the creative potential of people and places.

Nancy Duxbury, PhD is the Executive Director of the Centre of Expertise on Culture and Communities, a three-year research project on cultural infrastructure in Canadian cities and communities, and an Adjunct Professor in the School of Communication, Simon Fraser University. She is a member of Metro Vancouver's Regional Culture Committee, and a former member of Statistics Canada's National Advisory Committee on Culture Statistics and the Canadian Cultural Observatory's Advisory Council.

She was a co-founder and Director of Research of the Creative City Network of Canada, a national non-profit organization that operates as a knowledge-sharing and professional development resource in the field of municipal cultural policy, planning, and practice. Prior to this, she was Cultural Planning Analyst at the City of Vancouver's Office of Cultural Affairs, and also served as Assistant Editor of the *Canadian Journal of Communication*.

She holds a doctorate in communication and a master's in publishing from Simon Fraser University, and has published nationally and internationally. Her research has focused on the involvement of municipalities in cultural development, cultural indicators, cultural infrastructure, culture and sustainability, cultural policy, and Canadian book publishing.

Other Publications
From Municipal World

To order any of the following Municipal World publications, contact us at: mwadmin@municipalworld.com, or 519 633 0031 (888 368 6125).

By-law and Question Voting Law – Item 1288

Candidates and Electors – Item 1219

Deputy Returning Officers Handbook – 1280

Electing Better Politicians: A Citizen's Guide (Bens) – Item 0068

Guide to Good Municipal Governance (Tindal) – Item 0080

How to Campaign for Municipal Elected Office (Smither/Bolton) – Item 1284

Making a Difference (Cuff) - Vol. 1 – Item 0059-1 and Vol. 2 – Item 0059-2

Measuring Up: An Evaluation Toolkit for Local Governments (Bens) – Item 0061

Municipal Election Law – Item 1278

Off the Cuff: A collection of writings by George B. Cuff - Vol. 1 (Cuff) – Item 0055-1

Ontario's Municipal Conflict of Interest Act: A Handbook (O'Connor/Rust-D'Eye) – Item 0050

Ontario's Municipal Act - codified consolidation – Item 0010

Open Local Government 2 (O'Connor) – Item 0030

Procurement: A Practical Guide for Canada's Elected Municipal Leaders (Chamberland) – Item 0070

Public Sector Performance Measurement: Successful Strategies and Tools (Bens) – Item 0060

Run & Win (Clarke) – Item 0020

Stepping Up to the Climate Change Challenge (Gardner/Noble) – Item 0095

Strategic Planning: A Users' Guide (Plant) – Item 0085

Truth Picks: An Observation on this Thing called Life (de Jager) – Item 0090